GEORGE SANDERS,
ZSA ZSA,
AND ME

GEORGE SANDERS, ZSA ZSA,

and me

David R. Slavitt

NORTHWESTERN UNIVERSITY PRESS

EVANSTON, ILLINOIS

Northwestern University Press
www.nupress.northwestern.edu

Copyright © 2009 by David
R. Slavitt. Published 2009 by
Northwestern University Press.
All rights reserved.

Printed in the United States
of America

10 9 8 7 6 5 4 3 2 1

Library of Congress Cataloging-in-
Publication Data

Slavitt, David R., 1935–
    George Sanders, Zsa Zsa, and
    me / David R. Slavitt.
        p. cm.
    ISBN 978-0-8101-2624-4
    (pbk. : alk. paper)
    1. Slavitt, David R., 1935–
    2. Film critics—United States—
    Biography. 3. Sanders, George,
    1906–1972. 4. Gabor, Zsa Zsa. I.
    Title.
    PN1998.3.S5858A3 2009
    791.43092'2—dc22
                        2009018144

∞ The paper used in this
publication meets the minimum
requirements of the American
National Standard for Information
Sciences—Permanence of Paper
for Printed Library Materials,
ANSI Z39.48-1992.

For Janet

"... the impulse which leads me to a Humphrey Bogart movie has little in common with the impulse which leads me to the novels of Henry James or the poetry of T. S. Eliot. That there is a connection between the two impulses I do not doubt, but the connection is not adequately summed up in the statement that the Bogart movie and the Eliot poem are both forms of art. To define that connection seems to me one of the tasks of film criticism, and the definition must be first of all a personal one. A man watches a movie, and the critic must acknowledge that he is that man."

—ROBERT WARSHOW,

THE IMMEDIATE

EXPERIENCE

GEORGE SANDERS,
ZSA ZSA,
AND ME

THIS IS TRUE. GEORGE SANDERS,
the actor, had an Uncle Sasha whom he remembered
from the old days in St. Petersburg. The uncle had
spent much of the revolution lying in a great carved
bed with a .22 pistol beside him on the coverlet that
he would, from time to time, use to shoot flies that
had landed on the ceiling to eat the jam his footmen
had smeared there. They stood by while he did this,
ready with champagne, extra rounds of ammunition,
and orange marmalade and strawberry jam—either
for him or the flies.

I read this a month or two ago and stopped as
one does sometimes, not merely to consider this odd
scene but to ask myself why it spoke to me and what
it suggested about how things are. It does invite a
certain degree of compassion for a man so driven by
boredom or disgust as to while away his mornings
in this fashion. The gunshots would not have been

particularly noticed—there was a revolution going on outside, after all. And the footmen must have been accustomed to the eccentricities of these extravagant people. One does not, in this instance, want to be a fly on the wall, but the scene persists in the imagination, its fixative being the knowledge that Sanders, some years later, committed suicide in a resort hotel in Barcelona, leaving behind a note to explain that he was doing this because he was bored.

The uncle and the nephew are different, of course. Sanders had an odd, oddly attractive career as a movie star, which he did not take seriously, from which he derived little satisfaction, and for which, toward the end, he felt a good deal of contempt. And while his disgust may have had its psychiatric dimension, it nevertheless invites an aesthetic or even a philosophical reading. It is a more interesting end, in any event, than that of his Uncle Sasha, who made his way eventually to London, where he became a professional houseguest until his welcome wore out. He wound up in France, on the Riviera, where, reportedly, he died of syphilis.

I have never been to Barcelona. I may never get there. I used to think I might want to go to see the Frank Gehry museum. But there is a Frank Gehry building MIT put up last year within walking distance of my apartment. I went by to take a look. And didn't like it much.

Of course, there are also those Gaudi buildings in Barcelona. I've seen pictures of them. Which may have to do.

It would hardly be worth a trip there to see the hotel in which Sanders killed himself on April 25, 1972, with a bottle of vodka and a hoard of Nembutal that he'd saved up. It was, his friend Brian Aherne says, "a small hotel overlooking the sea," which sounds nice, but obviously wasn't nice enough. It was actually outside Barcelona in Castelldefels, at the Hotel Don Jaime, which is nice enough but is up on a hilltop, so that it overlooks the sea from some distance. Pool, sauna, sundeck, and all the standard amenities, but it's part of the Clarion chain, which doesn't suggest glamour.

But who needs to go there, when one can lie in bed, stare at the ceiling, and imagine it well enough? No jam, no flies, no bullet holes, but it is an adequate screen on which to project whatever mental movie the home office sends.

Those footmen are interesting. Vladimir and Piotr, let's call them. They are worried not so much about their lunatic employer as by the occasional crack of gunfire outside, for they understand that if the revolution succeeds, they will have to find other, and almost certainly more arduous, work. With fewer perks, like the undrunk champagne, for instance, with which they congratulate themselves for having satisfactorily served their quirky master for yet one more day. I can even see them taking a kind of pride in his nuttiness. Sane employers with reasonable demands do not test the loyalty or manners of their servants. It is only in situations such as theirs that excellence can demonstrate itself, as it is only in rough weather that a well-built vessel shows its seaworthiness.

I have had cleaning women and once, for a little while, a cook. But never footmen.

It would be pleasant if, in the course of these musings, Vladimir and Piotr were to follow me about, offering conveniences and comforts, and even doing some of the heavy lifting of transitions and scene setting.

It wasn't merely boredom, of course. Sanders was ill, had some sort of microhemorrhage of the cerebellum, or more bluntly, a small stroke. He couldn't speak properly and therefore couldn't work anymore. Even if he disliked his profession and, in his disillusion, preferred bad parts in dreadful movies toward the end of his career, he would have been frightened at least a little by the diminution in his earning power. His rather less wifty and more moving explanation: in a letter he sent to Aherne, he refers to Auden's remark that "life is a process whereby one is gradually divested of everything that makes it worth living, except the gallantry to go on. Well, screw the gallantry."

★

His ailment was diagnosed at Mass General, which is the one I use. It is, when the weather is fine and I am feeling healthy, within walking distance, just a bit farther than the Gehry building. An extravagant kind of fellow, Sanders would most probably have been in the Phillips House, high up with great views of the river on one side or of Beacon Hill on the other. (The windows are sealed, so as to prevent patients from jumping.)

But as Sanders demonstrated, there are other ways to go. He was a few months shy of sixty-six.

I'm older than that.

He had won an Oscar for best supporting actor for his performance as Addison DeWitt, the critic, in *All About Eve,* which won the best picture award, and many others, that year. Sanders played a witty, debonair, caddish fellow with no morals but elegant manners. He brings Marilyn Monroe to a party. She is Miss Caswell, whom DeWitt introduces as a "graduate of the Copacabana School of Dramatic Art." I was a critic for a while. But although I have a white silk scarf like the one he wears in the film, I wasn't like that. Acerbic, sometimes, but never DeWitty. Never the avenging devil, as Sanders was, threatening to expose the lies of the aspiring Phoebe and blackmailing her into bed. Not that

I was always above some abuses of power, but I wasn't altogether a bounder.

Sanders didn't mind that, enjoyed it even, and his offscreen character was pretty much what we saw in the films. His autobiography is called *Memoirs of a Professional Cad.*

In the last few years of his life, he was in some monumentally dreadful pictures. Have you ever heard of *Doomwatch?* Sanders was in it, playing the Admiral. It's a sci-fi turkey in which the people on an island are affected by chemical dumping, so that by eating contaminated fish they turn into cannibalistic mutants. *Endless Night, Psychomania,* and *Appuntamento col disonore* were his three flicks before that.

Miss them if you can.

He liked these movies because he never had to worry about his performance. All he had to do was show up. Or at any rate, that was what he said, so as to sound content.

Eventually, even showing up became too burdensome.

The difficult thing about acting is that you have to be there with your body, which is, whether you mean it or not, a kind of investment. He tried to separate himself from what he was doing, to accept the limitations of the situation, to take the money, put in the time, and leave, but it isn't easy. Your body is there, and your mind is in its little bone box, and hiding somewhere (or trying to hide and failing), your soul is there, too. It would be less difficult if it were more demanding, but as I discovered when I was a flicker picker, most of the time the performers just hang around, waiting for the lights to be set up or for some other technical wizardry to be performed. They have trailers or dressing rooms, places to go and sit in private—but the sitting is the hard part, because how can they not think about what they've just done or are about to do? And sometimes they have to do it over and over again, knowing each time that it's stupid, stupid, stupid, but unable to change a thing.

I have a couple of sweaters my ex-wife knitted from patterns that Natalie Wood gave us. She liked to knit between takes but was impatient, so she used knitting needles the size of telephone poles. This makes for a very coarse, open fabric, but the progress is visible. The action on the set might have been agonizingly slow, but the sweaters progressed like crazy, and she could see them growing on the needles.

Sanders didn't knit, although the sad truth is that knitting didn't do Natalie much good.

But the Oscar? Wouldn't that have helped? On the contrary, the memory of that achievement—his and not his, because those witty lines he was delivering were by Joseph Mankiewicz, after all—would have been burdensome. Any recollection of that performance, however fleeting, would only have aggravated his feelings of disgust. What a dizzying comedown!

I know a little about comedowns, myself. I had a couple of best sellers, thirty-some-odd years ago. One of them sold four million copies. These days, I am taking the high road, partly because it is distressing to write potboilers, and I may not have the stomach for it anymore, but mostly because my kids are out of college, and I don't need large sums of money. So I don't have the incentive.

What in the world has this to do with George Sanders? Not an awful lot, but I do remember what it was like to show up, to sit down at the desk each morning, to endure again the trauma of exerting myself in an effort to do something fundamentally pointless, and to do it frankly and confessedly for the money, just because the public is less well educated than I am and prefers kitsch to art, *poshlost* to the real thing.

So when I think of him and those terrible movies, I feel some connection, some recognition. Not that I am at all suicidal, but I am sympathetic to his predicament. I share his disgust. But Piotr and Vladimir do not show up with their jam pots, champagne bottles, and bullets.

So one must improvise.

What movie stars are for, after all, is to provide an iconography for our private lives. From their enlargements, distortions, and simplifications, we find a kind of clarity.

Heidegger, Husserl, and Merleau-Ponty are not the philosophers for the masses, nor even Ortega y Gasset. Those are Bruce Willis and Tom Cruise and Julia Roberts. We project. Or more accurately, we ingest, find our representatives, and incorporate them, taking what we can of their styles and stances as a way of facing the vicissitudes and opportunities of life. This is why *People* and all those lesser fan magazines have flourished for so long. It may be burdensome to the movie actors, I imagine, but then, they are compensated well enough so that they ought not to complain.

My models hardly exist anymore. The older, dapper guy, the experienced fellow who, from time to time, rouses himself from his cynicism—Adolphe Menjou, James Mason, Louis Calhern, William Powell, David Niven, Ronald Colman . . . or George Sanders. Where are their equivalents today?

The centenary of Jean Gabin's birth was 2004. Late in 1993, I saw, for the first time actually, *Touchez pas au grisbi,* a wonderful film that Jules Dassin remade as *Riffifi,* which was almost as good. Gabin was just brilliant—suave, world-weary, poised, but in the end fated for disaster. Which of us is not, after all? I looked up his other pictures to see what else there might be that I'd never seen and saw his birth date: May 17, 1904. I proposed to several magazines of some seriousness that deign from time to time to notice movies that I should do a piece about Gabin's career to mark the occasion. Nobody was interested. Not a one. (And some of these hotshot editors needed me to explain to them who Gabin was!)

I was appalled but not surprised. After all, my ex-agent reported to me once that an editor at Knopf wanted to know from what language I was translating the Psalms of David.

Nobody knows anything anymore, as Sanders had perhaps figured out.

Imagine, if you will, a musical version of Hannibal crossing the Alps. A joke, right? No, in fact they did this with Esther Williams and Howard Keel, for God's sake, and Marge and Gower Champion. And as Caesar Fabius Maximus, a man dominated by his mother and just a little faggy, George Sanders! There is such a movie: *Jupiter's Darling*, MGM, 1955. It's out on DVD, and you can look at it. Sanders had a song in it, which he sang so well in his bass-baritone voice that they cut it, because it wasn't faggy enough.

Yes, sure, he got paid, but when Marge and Gower Champion's dance number about elephants stays in and your number winds up on the cutting-room floor because it's too good, then you have to wonder what obtains.

He probably never saw the film. It was his habit to avoid them if he possibly could.

It is only slightly awkward to be writing about a movie star I never met, but it is more accurate, more representative. How many ordinary people get to hobnob with film stars, after all? It is irrelevant. The parts they play in our lives do not depend on personal contact; it is a matter mostly of projection and fantasy. The actual human being has little to do with the transaction. Still, people ask what Albert Finney was like, or Audrey Hepburn or Marcello Mastroianni, mostly, I think, because they want to be reassured that they have not altogether been taken in, that there is some relationship between the Hepburn in their heads and the one I lunched with once in Rome.

Well, she was different from what you think—less fragile, tougher—and funnier than they let her be on-screen. Just as gorgeous, though, as you always thought. Maybe even more so, because we try to allow for the cosmetics and the cinematography and the lighting. But she didn't need them all that much. She was drop-dead beautiful. And playful.

John Hersey and his wife were at the lunch, and Barbara Hersey asked the weirdest question: "Where in Rome can one find a cat?"

A brief pause. Was it a setup for a joke? Was she serious?

Then Ms. Hepburn, in a perfectly serious tone, suggested, "You must call Anna Magnani. She breast-feeds them."

A beat. And then a wonderful, radiant grin.

I loved her!

But does that help you? Does it do anything more than confirm what you already thought and felt from *Roman Holiday* or *Two for the Road* or *My Fair Lady*? You have your own Audrey Hepburn, with those huge eyes and that splendid neck, and my brief encounters can do nothing but smudge that or drag me into it, which is not what you want.

At the press party before the opening of *My Fair Lady,* I found myself alone with her for a moment, and I asked her an aggressive question. I was a young ambitious kid on the make, and I wasn't going to be intimidated by any mere movie star. "Tell me," I said, "after Wendy Hiller's performance in *Pygmalion* and Julie Andrews' in the stage version of *My Fair Lady,* wasn't it a little bit scary to do this?" She looked at me for a moment, smiled ruefully, and said, "No, you don't understand. What would have been scary would have been to turn down the million dollars."

Truth? From a movie star? But that's what we ask of them, and only rarely do such opportunities arise when they can deliver themselves of it.

That wit of hers wasn't, at any rate, what the studios were selling. They were perfectly well aware that it would have frightened off a fair number of potential ticket buyers. And when they talk about the "industry," they aren't just being grandiose or self-congratulatory: money is the point of it.

"The dream factory" is another name they give themselves, and that's accurate, too, except that they're not our dreams but theirs, which are mostly of big dollars. Socko in Chi! Boffo in Cleve!

Audrey Hepburn was the first person I'd ever known who became a postage stamp. I bought a couple of sheets and use the stamps for letters to special friends. They are just a bit waiflike, with the huge eyes making her look sadder and more vulnerable than she was in person. It was her *Roman Holiday* look. She could have done lots worse, though. Red Warren, who was my teacher back at Yale, was similarly commemorated on his centenary, and his postage stamp looks quite unlike him—too young, too smooth, almost vague. Even so, I bought a sheet of those, too.

According to his friend Aherne, Sanders was pretty much the same offscreen as he was on, the main difference being that he had very little small talk, and there could be long silences when, if he had nothing in particular to say, he wouldn't say anything. This could be unnerving. One could even imagine it as hostile—which would not necessarily be incorrect.

A. J. Liebling once told me that one of the advantages of being fat was that his silences were heavier than those of other people. And interview subjects would do almost anything to avoid their awkwardness (as if an interview were a social occasion) and blurt out all kinds of intimate information that they might later regret having spilled. Sanders' silences could be weighty, too, either because they could be prolonged or because he was a big guy.

His autobiography is silent about his elder brother, Tom. Tom Conway, that is, who starred in ten Falcon movies and a couple of Bulldog Drummond pictures. They had decided that two movie actors named Sanders might be confusing, and they tossed a coin for it. George won and remained Sanders. Tom lost and became Conway. He died in 1967. Actually, on April 22, so George's suicide was within a couple days of the anniversary of Tom's death. This could have been purely coincidental, but psychiatrists have observed annual grieving, especially when there are unresolved issues between the grieving person and the deceased, as there were with these brothers.

Conway had become a hopeless, helpless drunk, and George had broken off relations with him. He may have been in the right to do this, but it still wouldn't have felt good. In 1965, some enterprising reporter—not me!—found Conway living in a $2-a-day flophouse in Venice, California, and wrote a tear-jerking feature about the former star. It brought in some gifts and contributions, but only for a while.

Where was Sanders? Why wasn't he helping? The weird story, which Zsa Zsa tells in *One Lifetime Is Not Enough*, her book with Wendy Leigh, is that some years earlier when Tom had been diagnosed as having cirrhosis of the liver and was told he was going to die, Sanders had given him forty thousand dollars and told him to go off to Capri where, if he was going to kick the bucket, he could do it with some style and in comfort. (And also far away.) Conway did go, and on Capri he met a German doctor of some sort who said that he had a serum that would either cure him or kill him. Either of these sounded attractive, and Conway tried whatever it was. And it cured him. Wonderful! But when he asked his brother George for more money, Sanders said, as Zsa Zsa reports, "I'm sorry old boy. You're my brother, but you're supposed to be dead. I never want to see you again."

It's what the Sanders character might do. The real (or decreasingly real) Sanders could do it, too, but less breezily, and it's not a wild surmise to think he might have felt some twinges of guilt, especially in April.

For the next couple years, Conway was in and out of the hospital. In April 1967, Zsa Zsa Gabor, who was now Sanders' ex-wife and was, therefore, Conway's former sister-in-law, visited him in his hospital room and gave him a couple hundred dollars, advising him to use it to tip the nurses so they'd be good to him. The next day, the hospital called her to say that he'd left with the money, gone to a girlfriend's house, and died in her bed.

Other than a bit part in *What a Way to Go!,* Conway's last film role was in *101 Dalmatians,* in which he was the voice of the collie. I took my son to see a screening of that. In 1961, he was four, and I think it was his first movie. They'd have given me a cast list and the publicity packet, but I don't remember noticing that Conway was in the picture.

More likely than not, he'd have been relieved for people not to have taken notice.

Zsa Zsa more or less attended at Sanders' suicide, too, almost as if she were a manifestation of the angel of death. Or no. In both cases, she was behaving well, doing what she could to make each of them more comfortable.

In April of 1972, Zsa Zsa was in London, shooting a dumb Frankie Howerd comedy called *Up the Front.* Benita Hume Colman Sanders—Ronald Colman's widow and George's third wife—had died in 1967, and George was on his own except for his sister, Margaret, and Zsa Zsa, his second wife, to whom he had been married for nine years. (He was later, very briefly, married to Zsa Zsa's sister Magda, but that had lasted only a month or so.)

Sanders came to see her, and she saw that he was in awful shape, looking sick and haggard, more depressed and sullen than ever. He was terrified of having another stroke that would reduce him even further, and he was depressed by his doctors' constraints—he wasn't allowed to drink anymore or to smoke. She was worried enough to take him to see a psychiatrist, which was the right thing to do. The psychiatrist agreed that Sanders needed help and urged Sanders to continue the visits, but he never did. He waited for Zsa Zsa to return to Los Angeles and then booked his flight to Barcelona.

It would have been a complicated encounter. One wants to be at one's best in the presence of an ex-wife. He'd have understood that she wasn't there to gloat, but it would have pained him to be such a mess and for her to see it. He'd been fond of her, even loved her, and he had been humiliated by her public entanglement with Porfirio Rubirosa. And what was worse was that now she was closer to him than anyone. Galling as it must have been to realize, she was all he had. Glad to see her? Yes, and even grateful, but one can feel gratitude and resentment at the same time.

I once saw Rubirosa playing polo at the Polo de Paris. He was rather diminutive, with a round, tanned face, and looked like a monkey. But he is said to have been hung like an elk. In classy restaurants in Paris, the waiters still refer to the huge peppermill as the "Rubirosa."

Zsa Zsa's affair with him, carried on in public as

it had been, was the occasion of the breakup of her marriage to Sanders.

Did Sanders know about her intervention with Tom? Let us give her the benefit of the doubt and assume not.

Even Sanders' booking the flight to Barcelona wasn't yet—or at least wasn't necessarily—suicidal. He couldn't stay long in London without losing his tax-exempt status, and taxes in the sixties were impossibly onerous. It could have been a decision he had to make, then, between following the advice of his psychiatrist or his accountant.

I was on *The Tonight Show* once, back when Johnny Carson was the host and it came out of New York. I was promoting one of my schlock novels, and I'd been booked into the show, had arrived, and had been bumped a couple of times already, because the slot for the writer was the last ten minutes. The show was an hour and a half back then, and if they ran long, the writer was sacrificed. A lesson for writers? Perhaps. Certainly on this third visit to 30 Rockefeller Plaza, the lesson I learned was that the place of a writer in America is to follow the encore of a singing dog. Some horrible act—Carson liked horrible acts if they were bizarre enough—preceded me, in which a guy with a Boston terrier that he held in his arms up close to his face sang "How Much Is That Doggie in the Window?" The dog would howl along—in pain, perhaps, or merely disapproval.

It cracked Carson up, and he had him do a second number, which cut into my time.

So I was just a bit jangled when I walked out there onto the stage. We had a more or less prearranged script, and Carson's first question to me was whether it was true that I'd written this book just for the money. To this I replied, as had been planned, that, as Dr. Johnson said, only a blockhead ever wrote except for money.

And Zsa Zsa, on the couch to my right, asked, "Who is Dr. Johnson?"

"A dermatologist on Eighty-sixth Street," I answered.

Carson laughed. We were off, I thought, to the races. And it was fun, except that I forgot to mention the name of my book, and my publisher was furious.

I was annoyed at Zsa Zsa for intruding and rattling me. But why not? The fiction was that we were in Carson's living room, having a conversation. It wasn't, at any rate, a hostile question. Her attempt to help Sanders was two years later.

Only now, thirty-five years on, do I realize that she was, in certain situations and within narrow limits, a wonderful person.

Unlike Tom Conway and George Sanders, I survived her attempt at assistance. I'm still alive.

In 1986, Zsa Zsa married her ninth husband,

Frédéric Prinz von Anhalt (but he is not really a prince and isn't from Anhalt). His name used to be Hans Robert Lichtenberg, and he bought his title of "prince" from an elderly German princess of Anhalt, who made her living with these kinds of transactions under the guise of an adoption— he was forty-seven years old. There have been no German titles of nobility assigned since 1919, and he is a prince the way Prince is a prince. At any rate, he and Zsa Zsa sued her daughter, Francesca Hilton, for stealing a couple million dollars by forging her mother's signature to take out a loan on Zsa Zsa's $14 million Bel Air house. The house was built by Howard Hughes and was once owned by Elvis Presley. Anhalt made the papers again when he claimed to be the father of Anna Nicole Smith's baby. And he sued the makers of Viagra, claiming that since he started taking their pills, he was impotent without them. (But then why would he have started taking the pills?) And more recently, he showed up in news photographs stark naked, wearing only a hat, and chained to the steering wheel of his Rolls-Royce Phantom. (Actually, Zsa Zsa's Rolls.) He explained his curious predicament with a story that would have been a joke in the writers' building in the old studio days. He said he had been stopped by three women, whom he assumed wanted to pose for a photograph with him. They mugged him at gunpoint and left him that way in the car. But as they learned back in those writers' conferences, stories don't really have to make sense. Who cares? And that exuberant irrationality has oozed out of the movies and crept over the landscape. Like kudzu. These kinds of things happen out in Beverly Hills.

The writers' buildings were a pocket of hell that Dante couldn't have imagined. Writers were—and are—necessary in the making of movies, but what they do is not highly esteemed. As Samuel Goldwyn once said, "Send over three or four people from the writers' building, and I can write it myself!"

My pediatrician's brother was Sidney Buchman, the screenwriter. He did the second-to-last script of *Cleopatra* and had been out in Hollywood for years. The story I heard about him was how he managed to get himself fired off a Rin Tin Tin picture. It was better to be fired, in which case he could go back to his office in the writers' building and wait for another assignment, than to quit, in which event the paychecks would stop. For that reason it wasn't easy to get a studio producer to fire a writer. But Buchman was a man of enormous ingenuity, and he wrote a scene in which Rin Tin Tin carries a baby *into* a burning building. The producer called him into his office, said that Buchman didn't understand the gestalt of these things, and with regret, let him go. The hardest part would have been keeping a straight face for the thirty seconds it took to get out of the room.

★

A Yale classmate of mine lived in Malibu for a while. I remember him telling me that he once saw what he took to be a bear barreling down the Pacific Coast Highway, but then, as it got closer, he realized it was Joanne Woodward's flocked Volkswagen. Her what? He looked at me and smiled, affectionately but also condescendingly. What I didn't understand was that nothing makes sense out there. You just try not to look surprised.

Zsa Zsa's plight is sad and sordid although, I guess, not surprising. It's what happens when you get old. Things fall apart. Sanders was unwilling to tolerate this and excused himself.

In some ways, Zsa Zsa was the opposite of Sanders. He was, whether he admitted it or not, an actor, and he was offended by what the movies did to him and with him. Zsa Zsa didn't care. In 2004, she and Buster Crabbe were elected to the B-movie Hall of Fame. They mentioned, in particular, her appearance in *Queen of Outer Space,* but it doesn't matter. She was a celebrity, a personality who was more famous for her "dahlink" than for anything she ever said or did on-screen. She explained that that was easier than remembering people's names. Before Bianca Jagger or Cher or Madonna, she was out there herself, famous for her marriages and her affairs and, later on, for slapping that cop. She was one of the three weird sisters—Eva and Magda were the other two—but she was by far the best known, less for her acting than for who she was. Eva died of food poisoning in 1995. Magda died of renal failure in 1997. Their mother, Jolie, also died in 1997 at the age of ninety-seven. Zsa Zsa's age is difficult to determine, but she is well into her eighties.

The prince, to whom she has been married for twenty-two years now, is in his sixties. Whatever the sordid or poignant dynamics of that marriage, it has now endured longer than any of the previous eight. Zsa Zsa is partially paralyzed and, according to her daughter, not altogether in her right mind, not that the daughter's testimony is absolutely unimpeachable. Clearly, she and the prince don't get along. Each claims the other is a money-grubber. (These claims may both be true; they certainly are not mutually exclusive.) But it is difficult not to feel some sympathy for Francesca's resentment about having been turned away from the house on Mother's Day.

The rage Sanders felt in his last days, Zsa Zsa probably feels now—if she feels anything, that is. Shortly before he died, his sister Margaret visited him in Majorca and was shocked to see him hacking away at his grand piano with an axe. He'd dragged it out onto the lawn and was demolishing it in a frenzy. If he couldn't play it anymore, he didn't want it.

What he could have said, of course, was that the piano had been defying him, smiling at him with all those white teeth, inviting him, daring him to play it. But he couldn't. And wouldn't ever be able to again.

First the piano, then himself. But he was fastidious about it. He left two notes. There is the famous one that was addressed to the world, saying, "I am leaving because I am bored. I feel I have lived long enough. I am leaving you with your worries in this sweet cesspool—good luck."

The other was addressed to the hotel manager and shows a lot of style. It said that there was fifteen hundred dollars in his pocket to cover his expenses, and it asked that he telephone Sanders' sister in London.

THERE WAS A GEORGE SANDERS

movie on cable last night, and of course I turned it on. It was *From the Earth to the Moon*, and it was released in 1958, just a few years before I started reviewing. I'd never seen it before, and I thought it would be a treat to watch a Sanders picture, now that I'm writing . . . whatever this is.

I couldn't make it through more than the first twenty minutes. It was so agonizingly awful, so utterly unbearable, that I had to give myself and Sanders a break and turn to some other channel. It was directed by Byron Haskin and, with Sanders, featured Joseph Cotten and Debra Paget. It was, I assume, some sort of response to the Russians' Sputnik. It was adapted from the Jules Verne story, and Cotten is the inventor of "Power X," which is either a rocket fuel or atomic energy, and he and his colleagues in this sinister club, who have already made fortunes supplying arms to both sides in the American Civil War, are now going to cash in big-time by arming small nations that will be able to send rocket ships to distant major countries.

But the plot is not the important part. And the characterization, a series of stylized sneers and posturings that verge on Kabuki, is not important either. What is gripping and, at the same time, unbearable is watching competent actors dressed up in their silly costumes, saying these strenuously stupid things and doing what the script requires them to do. Haskin is probably best known for having directed *Treasure Island*, with Robert Newton chewing up the scenery in an amiable way, but by the time he got to this picture, he was merely doing his job, getting the scenes shot, and not giving more of a damn than it was worth.

It is wearing, corrosive to the spirit. I never met Haskin, wouldn't know him from Adam's off ox, but I once had drinks with King Donovan, a man of some obvious refinement who had been in the Hollywood jungle for too long and had gone native. He'd directed *Promises, Promises,* an altogether worthless piece of soft-core porn notable only for the relatively brief and shamelessly irrelevant nude appearance of Jayne Mansfield.

You remember Jayne Mansfield? She was one of those sex goddesses of the sixties, married to Mickey Hargitay, the bodybuilder. She died in 1967, when her car crashed into a truck in Slidell, Louisiana, and she was decapitated.

Promises! Promises! was not a film to be proud of, but I'd accepted an invitation from Honest Jet Fore to come and have a drink with Tommy Noonan, Ms. Mansfield's costar, and King Donovan, the director. And I'd been told that Honest Jet Fore was a character and that I'd find him fascinating. He was the kind of guy who fixed things. When he was working for Fox, he was told that Louella Parsons had asked the head of the publicity department to organize a ceremony at the gravesite of her late husband on the anniversary of his death. Her husband had been in the military, although it wasn't clear that he'd ever actually been in combat. But she was such a power in Hollywood that the head of publicity agreed instantly, hung up, took another antacid, and called Fore, instructing him to deal with it.

Fore went to the costume department and got himself outfitted in an army uniform complete with rifle. He then called Louella to tell her that the ceremony would be on Thursday at three o'clock. When that day rolled around, he went up to the cemetery at a quarter of three, shot off a few blanks, scuffed up the turf, and stood at attention, waiting for Ms. Parsons to arrive. Just before three, she was driven up. She got out of her car, looked around, and saw Fore standing there in an army uniform—all alone. Where is the ceremony, she wanted to know.

He told her how lovely it had been. There were twenty soldiers, a drummer and a bugler, flags, and the chaplain of the Fox VFW post, who had said some wonderful things. He gave her a sheet of paper on which he'd written out what the chaplain ought to have said.

"But where are they?" she wanted to know.

"It was at two o'clock. We waited as long as we could, but they had to get back."

"Three! You said three!" she insisted.

"No, no. Two! I'm sure. It was wonderful. It was a shame you missed it."

What could she do but take the piece of paper, shed a tear, get back into her car, and drive away?

Fore waited until she'd driven off, and then he went back to Fox and turned in the uniform and the rifle.

How could I not listen to whatever he was pitching—even *Promises! Promises!*? I met him and Noonan and Donovan in a bar on Sunset Strip. It was ten thirty or so in the morning. And Donovan, a tall, distinguished fellow with one of those narrow saturnine faces, was obviously already drunk. I can't remember whether he wore an ascot, but he had the air of one who has ascots hanging from hooks in his closet. Fore, a more plebeian and somewhat pudgy fellow, had a cup of coffee. Noonan, Donovan, and

I each ordered a Bloody Mary. But by the time the waiter had brought the drinks, Donovan had put his head down on his arms on the table, fallen asleep, and started a series of gentle snores.

The constraints of civil life are such that Fore, Noonan, and I contrived somehow to overlook this quirkiness and carry on a more or less normal conversation, which we were able to do quite well for twenty minutes or so. But then Donovan picked up his aristocratic head, looked at me, pointed a long, bony index finger, and confided in me—the young critic who thought he knew it all—the valuable secret of his craft. "The thing is . . ." he said. "The thing is . . . you must never show the wooly-wooly." And he then put his head down on the table again and returned to dreamland.

Tommy Noonan, I discovered only recently, was John Ireland's half brother. Google turned that up. It also led me to a photograph of Noonan's grave at the San Fernando Mission Cemetery near Los Angeles. As if he were some kind of martyred saint who people thought could intercede for them. Certainly that martyr quality is what I associate with Jayne Mansfield. She and Kim Novak were less successful versions of Marilyn Monroe, although none of them lived lives any of us would want for ourselves or our daughters.

What gives *All About Eve* a macabre interest that Mankiewicz couldn't have intended, and probably wouldn't have wanted, is that it features three actors who killed themselves: Sanders, Marilyn Monroe, and Barbara Bates, who was Phoebe, the girl who is holding Eve Harrington's award in the last scene of the picture, looking at herself in the mirror, and clearly positioning herself to do to Eve what Eve has done to Margo Channing. Barbara Bates killed herself in her mother's garage in Denver in 1969.

On the other hand, who knows what Mankiewicz knew or intended? I interviewed him once, and although we were supposed to be talking about *Cleopatra,* he was much happier with any other subject. *All About Eve,* for instance. And he told me that he'd had a hell of a time getting the studio to let him use Monroe, because to do that, they had to extend her contract. She had been hired as a comfort girl for the visiting New York executives, and she had, until then, appeared in only a couple films: *Love Happy,* a late, lame Marx Brothers picture they made to pay off Chico's gambling debts, and *The Asphalt Jungle,* a terrific John Huston heist movie with Sterling Hayden, Louis Calhern, and Sam Jaffe. Johnny Hyde, Marilyn's agent, had somehow persuaded Mankiewicz to look at *The Asphalt Jungle,* which was enough to get him to want her for Addison DeWitt's date. But the Fox executives thought it was ridiculous and embarrassing for Mankiewicz to want to use her as an actress, and he had to insist.

She was very grateful, Mankiewicz explained to me. Hyde had a heart attack, and she went to visit him in the hospital, where she thanked him so strenuously that he died.

I remember the look on Mankiewicz's face, a bugging of those astonishingly piercing blue eyes and, at the same time, a pained grin. And let's face it, it's funny. It's as good a way to go as any—being blown away by Marilyn Monroe.

But there is also the other, larger part of it, which is that she had, in this anecdote and in *All About Eve,* too, signaled her odd role in the society, which is more or less that of the temple prostitute, the holy whore who gives herself to the goddess and all comers in a quest for . . . immortality? Well, she has that. But that isn't it. A kind of wisdom? An engagement with reality that the rest of us would not dare and can scarcely imagine?

What I didn't tell Mr. Mankiewicz was that I'd been at her wedding in 1956, in White Plains, when she married Arthur Miller. True. Miller's agent was Kay Brown, whose husband was a lawyer in White Plains and knew my father. Either he or Kay Brown called my father to ask him to help figure out a way to get to White Plains from Miller's house in Ridgefield and to plan a place where Miller and Marilyn Monroe could get married without the reporters and photographers all over them. My father proposed a series of back roads and suggested that they use the county courthouse and come in the back way where the sheriff generally delivered prisoners. He offered them Judge Arthur Brennan's chambers, where Seymour Rabinowitz, a city court judge in White Plains, could actually perform the ceremony.

Okay, except that this seemed to my mother very dreary. A civil ceremony in a judge's chambers? "Even Marilyn Monroe deserves a glass of champagne."

The "even" is telling. It expresses my mother's discomfort, her feeling that Marilyn Monroe was not quite a member of our species. Mother's standards were such that, when she had to obtain a copy of the *Daily News* or the *Daily Mirror* that my father might need, she had the newspaper dealer put those papers in a brown bag so that she would not be seen carrying them on the streets.

But who was to get champagne and glasses and a tray? Me! I had just graduated from college and was available. I was dispatched to run these errands and recruited to serve as the bartender. I did as I had been told.

(Ah, you see? Piotr and Vladimir? *Mes semblables. Mes frères.*)

Judge Rabinowitz performed the ceremony. In attendance were Arthur, Marilyn, Arthur's cousin Morton Miller and his wife, Florence, Marilyn's photographer and friend, Milton Greene, my mother and father, and me.

Judge Rabinowitz: I now pronounce you man and wife.

Arthur and Marilyn kiss.

Marilyn (in that characteristic breathy squeak): So, we're married.

Arthur: So, let's go home. Mama has a chicken.

My mother signals to me, and I step forward with the tray of champagne glasses I've borrowed from Times Jewelers. But I stop. Because Morton, Judge Rabinowitz, and my father are kissing Marilyn. Will I miss an opportunity like this? Of course not. I put down the tray, and I, too, kiss her, a chaste peck but a real kiss, so that I can tell my grandchildren, honestly, that I kissed Marilyn Monroe.

Then I pick the tray up and serve the champagne.

She was sexy, of course, but not gorgeous. I remember that she was wearing a sweater and a butt-sprung skirt. Her face was dead white, although one could see that the bones were great and that it could conceivably be made to look wonderful for the cameras with the right makeup and lighting. She had that waiflike quality that was part of her appeal.

I think that was what my mother had responded to and what had prompted her to send me out for the champagne to make it just a little less bleak.

And if there was a kind of compassion my mother felt for her, there was also a degree of admiration in Mankiewicz's account of her early days at Fox—that she was such a poor pincushion creature kept around for New York executives to fuck, that he was almost prevented from using her as an actress. What he admired was that she had been able to put up with it, to survive it, to accommodate. And if it killed Hyde, that was too bad, but she was only doing what she'd learned to do.

In one of the canned bios that Google turned up, I read that Prince Rainier had thought about marrying her before he settled on Grace Kelly. And what I'd heard about Grace Kelly was that she'd been known to fuck a headwaiter to get a good table. I can't remember who it was who told me this, but whoever it was admired her for her single-mindedness, her lack of sentimentality, her dedication.

In *All About Eve,* Miss Caswell isn't just there as Addison DeWitt's sex toy, remember. He has had her, of course, but he is doing her a favor, bringing her along so as to introduce her to Max Fabian (Gregory Ratoff), a producer whom she wants to "meet" for the chance of maybe getting a part in one of his productions.

This is how Mankiewicz was characterizing the business of the theater. And movies, as he and his brother Herman knew, are even worse.

If DeWitt is not doing this service for Miss Caswell out of the goodness of his heart, it is at least a fair deal, and both parties have agreed to the bargain. His blackmailing of Phoebe at the end of the picture is less attractive, exploitive, and just a bit nasty—the intention being perhaps to balance the female nastiness of Eve Harrington, and presumably Phoebe as well, by a show of male misbehavior. It makes sense in the film, and Sanders is persuasive, because that is generally his on-screen character. He is cynical and world-weary and ruthless.

He has knowledge—that Phoebe is a liar and has never been to San Francisco, where she claims to have performed in the Shubert Theater, which DeWitt knows does not exist—and he turns that knowledge into power, which is corrupting. I had a little power myself, being the third most important movie critic in the world when I was doing it, in terms of box office impact—after only Bosley Crowther at the *New York Times* and Brad Darrach at *Time.* Mostly I used, or even abused, my clout in relatively innocent ways, because it was fun. The studio executives were thugs anyway. I remember when Warner Brothers yanked all their ads from the *Herald Tribune,* because they thought Judith Crist's review of Delmer Daves' dreadfully saccharine *Spencer's Mountain* was too harsh. The *Trib* was losing money, and Warner Brothers thought that it would therefore be vulnerable to that kind of thuggery.

So when I could stick it to one of the major moguls, I was delighted to use my invulnerability. (*Newsweek* didn't have any movie ads, after all.)

I couldn't do anything to Jack Warner, but an opportunity did arise for me to zots the head of Twentieth Century Fox. I remember a sentence I wrote about Irina Demick's appearance in *The Visit,* for whom a part was written in to please Darryl Zanuck: "Only Darryl Zanuck would have the Medicean chutzpah to turn a play by one of the leading German-language dramatists of our time into a vehicle for his doxy who can neither stand, sit, nor presumably, lie down convincingly." Excessive, maybe, but true enough, and it had an Addison DeWitt sneer that I was trying on and still find myself using from time to time. It also got me banned "for life" from Fox screenings.

Not a terrible worry, actually, because I had already decided to give up movie reviewing. It wasn't a serious job for a grown-up. My kids were going off to school to learn to read and write, and I was taking the train into New York City, wearing a suit and tie and looking like all the other serious people on the train platform, except that they were going to law offices and jobs in banks, while I was going to see an Annette Funicello movie, and that seemed . . . silly!

But to show Fox that I wasn't altogether their victim, I bought a ski mask from the Ski Shop of Saks Fifth Avenue and got a ticket from a friend at *Life,* so I could disguise myself and sneak into the press screening of *The Sound of Music.* And then, on the way out, without the ski mask anymore, I smiled at Mort Segal, the "director of world publicity" as his letterhead proclaimed, and watched him turn ashen.

I panned that one, too. "Austria: The Last Golden Days of the Thirties" is how the opening title read, and I asked whether anybody had ever heard of the Depression or *Anschluss* and continued from there. But I didn't hurt the picture any.

I'd had problems with Fox and vice versa. They'd invited me on a junket for "out of town reviewers," and I had accepted, not as the *Newsweek* guy, because we weren't allowed to take such goodies, but as the *Yale Review* movie reviewer, which I also was. They took a planeload and busload of people to Salzburg for *The Sound of Music,* to Viareggio and Rome for *The Agony and the Ecstasy,* and to London for *Those Magnificent Men in Their Flying Machines.* At Viareggio, I'm afraid I behaved less well than they'd have liked. We were supposed to go to Forte dei Marmi to see them blow up a huge piece of marble, and the bus left early in the morning. I said that if God meant for me to go see that, he wouldn't have put me on a beach where I could look out at the Bay of Spezia and contemplate the death of Shelley.

They were sufficiently pissed off to have some upper-middle executive rat me out to the management at *Newsweek,* where Gordon Manning chewed me out and explained, as if talking to a half-wit, that this was why they had the rule. These aren't nice people. Finally, the penny dropped, and I realized that Gordon was right. But if they weren't nice people, that meant I didn't owe them anything.

What I remember is standing in the Sistine Chapel with a lot of other reporters, reviewers, and columnists who were gathered around Charlton Heston. Some fawning woman suggested that Heston really resembled Michelangelo. Mostly, I had been keeping my mouth shut, but this was too absurd, and I said, "Michelangelo was five feet six inches!" (That may or may not be true.) Heston, who was six feet three, glared at me and said, "In my book, Michelangelo was one of the tallest men who ever lived." It was so zany as to be endearing.

Our powers—mine and those of my colleagues—were limited. We could help a small foreign movie, but we couldn't do much to hurt a picture with a huge advertising and publicity budget.

I could hurt people's feelings, though. I used to dump on Suzanne Pleshette with particular venom whenever I possibly could. I could have ignored *A Distant Trumpet,* but it was an occasion to talk about her shortcomings and even to make catty remarks about her looks, which I did because she had once lived in the same apartment building as my ex-wife, and they had ridden down in the elevator together, and my ex-wife would say hello or good morning, and some days Ms. Pleshette would answer and some days not. What husband wouldn't take advantage of a chance to avenge such discourtesies?

She never knew why or, probably, who. I was the unit chairman of the Newspaper Guild, and I was the one who kept the names off the reviews. Out of vanity as much as anything else. I didn't want copy that other people had messed with to appear over my name. But up in the front of the magazine, in nine point pearl, my name appeared as the movies editor. And people in the business knew who I was. Even so, she'd never have made the connection and could not possibly have imagined that her rudeness, so many years earlier, was coming back to bite her in her ample ass.

I never did her any permanent harm, though. She went on to find a more congenial medium in sitcoms on TV, divorced Troy Donahue, and eventually married Tom Poston. I wished them well. And when she died, I had a twinge—but only a twinge—of regret about what I'd done to her. But it's probably not going to be what I'll be kept out of heaven for.

There were occasions when I could do a movie some good, and I was happy to call attention to accomplished or amusing films that had slipped through the cracks or to which other critics hadn't paid enough attention. *The Raven* was one of these, a schlocky Roger Corman movie with Boris Karloff,

Peter Lorre, and Vincent Price. From American International, which was, by itself, a disadvantage. This wasn't art, but then it wasn't trying to be. And even though Gertrude Lawrence's word hadn't yet come into general circulation, I was confident enough in my own judgment and reactions to know that these pictures were camp, which is to say good bad movies. Their lack of pretensions recommended them. And I would give them long, almost ecstatic notices, hoping that I could get my readers to share my delight in them. Robert Warshow, one of the very few really good film critics we ever had, said in *The Immediate Experience* that one of the most difficult things a movie reviewer has to do is to admit that he was there. When I first read that, in the month before I took over the movie desk, I thought it was mysterious and gnomic, but I soon discovered what he meant. This is, for God's sake, an Annette Funicello beach-blanket movie, but as it unrolls before one's cynical eyes, one realizes that, as beach-blanket movies go, it's not at all bad. And you owe it to your readers, or at the very least to your own honor, to say so.

So I said so about *The Raven*, and Ruth Pollagee, the American-International publicist, thanked me by inviting me to lunch—with Peter Lorre and Boris Karloff. (Price was indisposed, I think, and couldn't make it.) A *grande bouffe* at the Four Seasons that went from one o'clock to a little after five, with great food and many expensive brandies. And I am there as the still relatively innocent, relatively young kid who can hardly believe his luck.

After several of those great, old brandies, Lorre explained to me how it was, the nature of things, and what he'd learned about life and art. "I was once a real actor," he said, in that famous savage whisper that combined menace, innocence, and self-loathing. "In the German edition of *Mann ist Mann* there is an afterword by Brecht, an appreciation of the art of Peter Lorre. And then Fritz Lang, that son of a bitch, turned me into a monster, and I have been playing monsters ever since." He gave me a baleful look and took another sip of his very expensive brandy.

He had become almost a joke. He was the model for Flattop in the Dick Tracy cartoon strip. He had appeared on radio programs and had been forced to exaggerate his odd speech patterns, because so many people had imitated him that he didn't sound Lorre-ish enough. For an actor to have to imitate caricatures of himself could not have been comfortable.

At least in the Corman movies, he had company, for Karloff and Price were men of a certain cultivation and refinement. These films were not demanding and were fun, and a not too horrible way to make a few dollars—although, now that I think of it, an American International production of a Roger Corman movie couldn't possibly have paid any of them very much.

★

What I admire about those guys now is their professionalism. To play a part in a good film may take talent, but to play as decently as possible in a turkey takes character, which also has its value in the world and which should be recognized. Lorre did several Mr. Moto movies, in which he was the eponymous Japanese detective. His accent wasn't particularly Japanese (more like the Andy Kaufman generic Foreign Man). But with a little makeup magic, he could pass for semi-Oriental. He was as much Japanese as Warner Oland was Chinese. Or Boris Karloff in the Mr. Wong series. What troubled Lorre about the Moto roles was that he was getting $10,000 a picture, while Oland, hardly in his class, was getting $40,000. That smarts.

Karloff's shtick in the Wong movies was that the backstory had him educated at Oxford, so he didn't have to do that bizarre pidgin. He could sound pretty much like Boris Karloff. The Orientalism was in his dressing gowns, his fondness for tea, and his general inscrutability. And some of the plots are clever enough so that one can look at the films without acute discomfort.

I see that Lorre's last two films, which he made shortly afterward, were *Muscle Beach Party*, an Annette Funicello/Frankie Avalon movie (but not even a good Funicello/Avalon movie), and *The*

Patsy, a Jerry Lewis picture. For some years, he'd had biliary colic, which is gallstone pain. I've had that. It's not fun. His doctor prescribed morphine for the pain. It turned him into a morphine addict. The morphine may have helped him through some of these films, though. He died of a stroke on March 23, 1964. March 23 is my birthday.

Sanders and Lorre appeared together in *Lancer Spy,* a spy flick of 1937 that Gregory Ratoff directed. The female lead—the star, really—was Dolores Del Rio. My guess is that Sanders and Ms. Del Rio had an affair, and that more likely than not, it was a way of amusing themselves during the filming. Their chemistry was good on-screen, too, and their next picture was *International Settlement,* another spy story, this one set in the Sino-Japanese War that was going on and embellished with newsreel footage of the bombing and fighting in Shanghai.

Toward the end of his life, Sanders had the bizarre idea of going to Mexico City, renewing his relationship with Ms. Del Rio, marrying her (she had a lot of money, and he had almost none), becoming a Mexican citizen, and, no kidding, running for the presidency of Mexico. He actually did go to Mexico City, but he didn't get more than a dinner or two from Del Rio. Instead, he came back to Los Angeles with a buxom young woman named Alberta (so he described her in a letter to Brian Aherne) with whom he took up residence for a week or so in one of the bungalows of the Beverly Hills Hotel. He wrote to Aherne that his new plan was to buy a houseboat and cruise the Rio Grande from El Paso to the Gulf of Mexico, so as not to be liable for taxes in either country.

The houseboat idea was a fantasy. But the other was real enough for him to go down to Mexico City, and . . . . Had he lost his mind?

Even now, after President Reagan and Governor Schwarzenegger, and Senator Murphy and Representative Sonny Bono, and with the idea of translating celebrity from the screen to the world of politics less absurd than it must have appeared then, it still seems outré.

He had had fantastic and delusional notions before, a couple of ventures into the world of business and finance that lost vast sums of money for his friends and investors. There was an engineering company and then, some years later, a sausage and provisions enterprise. Both were catastrophes because Sanders didn't pay attention, which is not a good thing to do in a start-up company. So, in a way, running for the presidency of Mexico was a less hazardous undertaking. At least, when he failed, no one was out of pocket. And if he'd succeeded? What difference could that have made? Most presidents of Mexico fail, some spectacularly. A few flee the country or are assassinated. Or both. Carranza, *por ejemplo.*

★

The thing about the movies is that they are all suppositional. It isn't just the films that are imaginary on-screen but also, more often than not, the deals for those films, the lunches, the treatments, the scripts in different colors of copy paper. People live in that limbo and, like cave-dwelling fish or insects that never see the light of day, lose their sense of sight, which is no longer useful to them. What we think of as reality is not only not a help but an actual hindrance.

That classmate I mentioned earlier sank into that swamp. He'd published a novel and then had been commissioned by Jerry Wald to work on a screenplay that would come out first as a novel and then, later on, Wald could make as a movie. With a not at all contemptible advance, he'd gone to Europe and lived it up for a while on the French Riviera, dancing at L'Esquinade Club in Saint-Tropez and having a good time. He even wrote a little. But the money ran low and then ran out. And no more was forthcoming from Mr. Wald. He wound up in Paris, living on stale hors d'oeuvres and elderly countesses. And then when that began to pall, he came back to the States and, with an allowance from his mother, set up light housekeeping in Los Angeles.

He made a little money writing short treatments. Producer A would buy the film rights to a book. Any book. It didn't matter much. A hundred thousand dollars, say, which was big money back then, only they didn't pay that. They paid maybe five hundred dollars. The rest was due on the first day of filming, which would never happen. Producer A could then hire my friend, or one of a hundred young men and women out there like him, to turn the book into a short treatment, an eight- to ten-page version of what the movie would be. And then Producer A could have a couple of lunches and hustle the "project" to another producer who would take it over and, if he was really hot for it, hire somebody to write the long treatment, forty pages or so. This they could resell to Producer C. Or even to a studio. Everybody could make a living, but nobody was making movies.

Crazy! But my classmate had his other plan, his "real" plan, which was to marry an actress with whom he was in love—and she might even have been fond of him. She'd married an aged producer with a bad heart, and the idea was that she'd fuck the producer to death and then marry my classmate, and they could live happily ever after on the money she'd inherit.

Except that the aged producer was no fool. He indulged in sex very rarely and kept nitroglycerine on the nightstand. He lived for years.

I don't think he ever hired my classmate to write treatments. He was beyond that. He made movies that actually showed in theaters. Not very good movies, maybe, but real ones.

During his time in Paris, my classmate used to go to Prince Feliks Yusupov's house now and then for dinner. He had no clear idea who the prince was or that he'd killed Rasputin. It was dinner. The prince had a still up on the roof, and he made his own vodka. And because he was a prince, when he drank, everybody else had to drink. And because he was a lush, he could drink everyone under the table. So by the time they all sat down at the dinner table, very few of the guests could eat anything, and a single chicken could feed a dozen people.

After dinner, they'd go up to the ballroom where there was a pipe organ, and according to my friend, someone would play sad Russian songs while the prince turned the pages of "the book," which was a catalogue of the jewels he'd given his wife when they got married. Here and there, a stone would be crossed out, and sometimes a whole piece. That was what they were living on. The prince would turn the pages and he'd cry, and all the guests would cry.

And Piotr and Vladimir would be standing by ready to refill glasses.

And then my classmate would walk halfway across Paris, climb up to his garret and fall asleep, and then, in the morning, try to work a little more on his novel.

It was only on the plane back to America, reading Robert Massie's *Nicholas and Alexandra,* that he found out who Yusupov was and how he'd poisoned, stabbed, shot, and finally drowned Rasputin.

It would have been about that same time that Sanders' Uncle Sasha was shooting the flies on the ceiling, sipping champagne, and waiting for the end to come.

I rented a 1946 Sanders movie recently that was probably his best performance—*A Scandal in Paris,* in which he plays Eugéne François Vidocq, a rascal and a thief who is redeemed by the love of a beautiful innocent and becomes the chief of police of Paris. It is a nonsensical picture, but it plays elegantly enough with a series of conventions in which Sanders is naughty but charming and his wickedness is redeemed by his wit. When, in the course of planning to rob their hostess, the Marquise De Pierremont, his low-life sidekick Emile (Akim Tamiroff) suggests that he may use his knife not only to pick the lock of the old marquise's bedroom but to kill her if she wakes up and cries for help, Vidocq reproves him with an elegance Oscar Wilde would have admired:

"I hope you're not suggesting violence," he says.

"Why not?" Tamiroff asks. "Are you beginning to grow moral?"

In his slightly nasalized, refined way, Sanders replies, "It isn't a question of morals but of manners. A man who is capable of killing with a knife is quite liable to eat with one."

How wicked can a fellow like that be?

That was Sanders' basic shtick, the portrayal of cynicism or even criminality that couldn't possibly be serious because he had such refinement. His face was so attractively sculptured as to be almost feminine. There is a feminine aspect to a great number of our tough guy heroes, after all. Think of Bogart's slight lisp or Jimmy Stewart's hesitations in speech that suggested a shyness that was nearly maidenly. Sanders was tall and commanding, but . . . pretty, and that excused a lot. It also signaled to the audience that he was redeemable, that even if he was planning to steal the jewels, there was hope for him, and as it turns out, the love of the young Therese (Signe Hasso) is going to pull him back from the brink of depravity. And when it does, we are not only taken in but delighted.

As he got older, that prettiness faded, and along with it the attractive moral iridescence. The declension was to elegant villainy, like that of Addison DeWitt, and then even the edge of that elegance began to dull. What is interesting, though, is that the conventions, the roles he had played, had begun to seem real to him. He was playing a part, not when he swallowed the pills and drank the vodka, but before that, when he wrote the note. It wasn't boredom he meant to complain about but despair. But could a Sanders character admit to such a thing? So he did what he had trained himself to do and left a note that might have been composed by one of those cartoon figures he had been playing for all those years.

On the news last night was an account of an altercation Tom Cruise had with some stooge for a British comedy show who had appeared at a London screening of *War of the Worlds,* held out a microphone, asked Cruise a question, and then . . . it turned out to be a joke microphone, and it squirted water in Cruise's face. He was furious. He wiped his face off with a towel some flunky had handed him and yelled at the prankster, "You think that's funny? You think that's funny? Why would you do that?"

The guy with the trick microphone didn't have the presence of mind to answer, "Yes, of course it is," or to tell Cruise he was lucky it hadn't been a pie, or to ask Cruise if, after having made all those movies, he still thought he was a real person.

But real people don't have flunkies standing by with towels, which is what I found puzzling. Had this been a setup? Was it all staged? Had Cruise been acting? That's what he does, after all.

The police arrested the man and his camera crew. But Cruise did not press charges.

There are said to be African primitives who think that the taking of a photograph will steal their souls. They may be right, but it takes a lot of photography to do it. The real person leaches away, and what is left is the image. It may happen to writers, too, but most of the time it is not so public a transformation.

3

WHAT THEY ARE, I HAVE COME

to realize, are whores. I don't even mean that in any pejorative way. If you want to be politically correct, we can call them sex workers, if you find that less offensive. But they have a lot in common with prostitutes, in that they learn to use their bodies in such a way as to convey emotions that they do not feel. Their bodies, moreover, are instruments of their craft. They look at themselves in their mirrors with a calculating and critical eye, and what happens eventually is that there is, for actors and actresses, an increasing distance between the body they see and the self that is looking, posing, and appraising. To some extent, we all are taught to do this, and we check our reflections in the glass before we leave in the morning. But the degree of refined attention that actors and actresses devote to face, figure, wardrobe, and maquillage is beyond us. It is not self-consciousness but, on the contrary, an assertion or, say, recognition of a self that is not that image in the mirror.

Their strenuous sex lives and frequent drug busts are, I shouldn't wonder, natural enough consequences of this disjunction. If that body is not "me," then why should I care who fucks it or whom it fucks, or what it snorts or smokes or puts in its veins? And this isn't the sole consideration either. There is also the huge money, which, very quickly, destroys their sense of proportion. There are the limousines, the luxury suites, the dresses from wardrobe, and the jewelry, all of which can dazzle away any idea of limitation. These trappings begin to seem natural and normal, and there is a sense of entitlement—that I can do whatever I want, whenever I want, and nobody can tell me not to, because the rules that apply to ordinary mortals cannot possibly apply to me.

That was what got Tom Cruise so angry in London. It wasn't just that he'd been squirted with water, but his face, that incredibly valuable asset, had been endangered. Only water? It would have taken him a few seconds before he was sure it hadn't been acid! It is, in no small part, that face that enables him to demand tens of millions of dollars to appear in a movie, and the face is worth it because it is a draw and, more likely than not, will earn back that amount and more at the box office.

If he owns the face, if it's an asset, then the

owner and the face can't be the same guy—which is what I take George Sanders to be talking about when he complains, in his autobiography, that he has had to have his teeth capped. He is no longer himself, no longer natural and authentic, and he feels a dissonance, the beginning of a divergence. He is walking around in a costume that extends now to include his own flesh and bone.

I think again, and perhaps more deeply, about that note of admiration I heard from Mankiewicz as he was telling me about Marilyn Monroe's stint as a studio whore. The ways in which women can separate themselves from their bodies and use their bodies as tools of their minds or their wills would recommend themselves to a director who is often in the position of telling them to project this emotion, kiss this man, embrace that one, show the camera a little more leg, take off your blouse and show us your tits, get in bed with him and pretend to have sex.

The Elizabethans did not allow women on the stage. That began with the Stuarts. The assumption was that, as between actresses and whores, there wasn't a lot of difference. They may have been right, not merely empirically but in a deeper way that has to do with this relationship between the body and the soul. Once that is disturbed, who are you? What are you?

It occurs to me that much of the fawning out there is a response to this desperate need many of these people have to be assured that they are who they are, that they are not impostors, that they are still, for whatever whimsical reason, the same people they were yesterday—still important, still bankable. That's what the flunkies are for.

I was out in Hollywood once with Freddie Brisson, who had optioned a play of mine that he wanted Otto Preminger to direct. A weird idea? Well, maybe, but Preminger had once been the head of the Theater in der Josefstadt in Vienna, had succeeded Max Reinhardt in that position, and had had that light touch of a Viennese pastry chef with the meringues of Molnár and Nestroy. My play, a version of *Romeo and Juliet* in which Friar Lawrence gets the girl, was that kind of confection. That Preminger had lost most of his *légèreté* during the course of his American moviemaking career seems not to have troubled Brisson, or if it did, he found reassurance in his basic strategy, which was, he told me, never to hire people who needed the money.

I remember being in Brisson's office when it became necessary for him to confer with Preminger on the phone. This must have been an afterthought, because we weren't in his private office but the outer one where the secretary sat, and she was placing the call. I remember that she got through to Preminger's secretary and then, in a move I'd never heard of before, suggested to her opposite number in Preminger's office, "Shall we ring together?"

This way, neither mogul would have to be in the humiliating position of being on the telephone and waiting for the other one.

Elaborate enough to have come from Saint-Simon!

Preminger was one of the few directors out there who had the clout and money to defy the studios. He could finance his own pictures, which gave him that freedom. He once told me that in Europe moviemaking is a little easier, because you can find a gangster of one kind or another who will back your film if you put his girlfriend in the film for three minutes. And all you have to do is shoot a scene in a restaurant where she is at the table behind the one at which your stars are eating. But in America? There are banks, but they are not interested in girls, and certainly not in art; all they care about is money. And movies are not predictable that way, or if they are, they aren't interesting.

Preminger could fight the censors—as he did with *The Moon Is Blue,* which used the word "virgin" for the first time on screen—or hire writers on the blacklist. And Brisson had produced *Five Finger Exercise* and *Under the Yum Yum Tree* and, on Broadway, *Coco,* and he was married to . . .

But wait. That's another story. I'd been warned, the day we first met, that he had a slight speech impediment, and my agent had told me not to react to it. I asked him what kind of a boor he thought I was. If he'd told me more, or if he hadn't told me anything, I'd have been okay, I think. But this was what I knew. I went over to the Columbia Pictures building on Fifth Avenue and went up to Brisson's quite large and handsomely outfitted office, shook hands, took the chair he'd indicated, and, maybe thirty seconds later, heard the door open behind me. I turned to see who it was, and Brisson said, "David, I'd like you to meet my wife, Wosalind Wussell."

I very nearly stifled the guffaw, but not quite enough. Brisson glared at me. And I knew, from that moment, that the play would never actually make it to Broadway.

Anyway, they knew who they were. The houses, the servants, the elaborate appanage of their lives confirmed for them every moment that they were movers and shakers, tastemakers, princes in the woefully Jacobin world of Hollywood. But in a paradoxical way, all that money and power that ought to be reassuring can turn burdensome, can attack rather than defend, and can pose from day to day, and even from hour to hour, the terrible questions: "Are you still worth this? Do you still deserve all this? What have you done lately?" And where, then, can these people turn for reassurance?

Well, when all else fails—as it almost always does—they turn to one another, which is to say that the name-dropping they indulge in is not at all casual but a pathological manifestation of their need to qualify. They are listing these names because to do so makes them feel better: if I know all these celebrities, I, too, must be somebody, right?

I remember the dinner party that Otto and Hope Preminger gave one evening when I was out there. They'd rented Frank Sinatra's house. (I know this, because either they told me or Freddie and Roz told me, or maybe all of them did.) I was down at the end of the table on Hope Preminger's left. Brisson was on her right. Otto was up at the head of the table, far, far away. And Brisson was going on about the Hansens, of whom I'd never heard. I asked him who they were, and he explained that they were the most wonderful couple. She was a fine cook and a practical nurse, and he was an especially thoughtful kind of butler who, during the movie after dinner, would go out and turn all the cars around so that they'd be pointing outward and the guests wouldn't have to jockey awkwardly.

(Piotr? Vladimir? Are you paying attention?)

They'd worked for George and Gracie Burns, but now that she'd died and he was living at the club, they were available, and he and Roz had been thinking of hiring them.

"Well, why ever not?" I asked.

"Yes, why not?" Hope asked.

"They're Danish," Brisson explained.

You sometimes get anti-Semitic Jews, but anti-

Danish Danes? They are less frequent. So, having been already classified as a boor and having nothing much left to lose, I asked, "And?"

Brisson explained that in Denmark on the king's birthday, everybody drinks a toast to the health of the monarch. In Hollywood, on the other hand, all the Danes get together at the Scandia to eat and drink for three days until nobody can even lie on the floor without holding on. And Hansen, he explained, was a friend of Lauritz Melchior, who brought him every year to these banquets.

"And?"

"And you can't sit with a man and drink for three days and nights and then come home and tell him to wash the mud off the hubcaps of the Bentley."

It's the kind of difficulty that we might imagine reading about in a Ronald Firbank novel, but that is only to say that it is exotic. The heads at our end of the table nodded in sympathy, or in hopes that they, too, might one day be faced with such a quandary. Or to acknowledge Brisson's membership in the select and almost otherworldly group that has to worry about such things.

Piotr and Vladimir would not have been amused.

Preminger would occasionally play some eccentric characters in films or even on television. He was Mr. Freeze in a couple of *Batman* episodes, replacing

George Sanders, who had been the original Mr. Freeze but then killed himself.

As far as I can tell, I am the only one from that dinner table who is still alive, and I tell their story not with derision—or, anyway, not only with derision—but with a degree of compassion. The house, the cars, the silver and china, the appurtenances of their lives were weightless, and they all knew it. Unless they were robbed by rapacious and crooked business managers, they were unlikely to lose everything, but that wasn't reassuring, or not reassuring enough. It was all flimsy, as temporary as if it had been lent by the properties and wardrobe departments. All that counted out there was reputation, the esteem of others, their places in the pecking order. Who waited for whom on the phone. It was even more ruthless than the court of the Sun King, because it was more whimsical. It was no more an aristocracy of talent than Louis' nobles and chevaliers were an aristocracy of valor and merit. Ultimately, box office clout was what supported them all, but the studio system blurred that and sometimes, for quirky reasons, ignored it.

What this meant was that their careers could not be separated from their private lives. There are two possible outcomes of this awkwardness. One is that for some actors, like Peter Sellers, the investment into the roles was such that, after a while, they lost track entirely of who they were. The other is more common—the character of the person and that of the roles begin to blur together, actors are cast to play what they have played before, what they seem like, and what they indeed are offscreen. That was, to some extent, Sanders' career, and it was most certainly Zsa Zsa's.

I found a DVD of John Huston's *Moulin Rouge* recently and watched it. It's not the worst movie ever made, and it has a couple of nice sequences of Toulouse-Lautrec's paintings and pastels. Not quite so good as what Kurosawa did with the "Crows" section of *Yume* (or *Dreams*), but nonetheless impressive. José Ferrer is not altogether laughable as Toulouse-Lautrec, even if he has some very mannered lines to deliver. But Zsa Zsa is . . . Zsa Zsa, playing herself mostly, although she is supposed to be Jane Avril. She has a couple of really bad songs to lip-synch (Muriel Smith, uncredited, did the actual singing) and some double entendre lines to deliver in an accent that suggests Budapest more than Paris. Mostly, she plays a classy courtesan, a gold digger with a little talent, conventional good looks, and most of all, an ability to make fun of herself that almost obliterates the unattractiveness of what she is doing.

Her only on-screen moment that breaks through the constraints of the film is at the end, in a strange way that John Huston could not have expected, but then artists do get credit for being right, whether or not they had any idea at the time about what they were doing. It is Toulouse-Lautrec's death scene, and in his final delirium in his bedroom back at his family's chateau, singers and dancers from the Moulin Rouge materialize to perform for him. Among these is Jane Avril—Zsa Zsa—who comes sashaying into the room with a great flourish to announce, in words she claims to have improvised herself, "Henri, my dear, we just heard you were dying. We just had to say good-bye. It was divine knowing you." She explains that she cannot stay: "There is the most beautiful creature waiting for me at Maxim's. Good-bye, Henri, good-bye."

It's the last line of the movie, and it strikes me as consonant with her odd angel-of-death farewells to Tom Conway and George Sanders, neither of which had yet played out.

A high-class tramp, then, whom we could think of as defiantly liberated except that she is a slave to wealth and celebrity. To read through *One Lifetime Is Not Enough* is to find a catalogue of great men she has fucked, from Kemal Atatürk, who, she claims, took her virginity, on down through three hundred pages of demoniac name-dropping. Some she went to bed with and tells about, and some she went to bed with but does not name. There were also some she declined, although their propositions—Prince Philip's, for instance, and Ali Kahn's and John F. Kennedy's—she records as trophies of a kind. As I guess they are. She is proud of her conquests. One of her tag lines is "How many husbands have I had? You mean, apart from my own?"

The worst of it is that one gets the feeling that, at least sometimes, the reason she boffed them was because of their names. They were objects for her collection, as she was, probably, for some of them. It wasn't the rumpy-pumpy but the mutual reassurance.

I read in this morning's tabloids the report that Princess Di and JFK Jr. had a one-night stand in a New York hotel and that JFK Jr. was definitely a ten in Diana's book—this from her friend and confidante, Simone Simmons, in *Diana: The Last Word* (which it almost certainly won't be). According to Ms. Simmons, Princess Di had dreams for a while of marrying him and becoming the first lady of the United States, which would have been even better, perhaps, than queen of England. (Does that make Sanders' idle thoughts of being president of Mexico look less foolish?)

We read of these absurdities with a little envy but also a little relief. How strenuously these people are driven, not by lust, let alone love, but by the need to know that they are important enough to have attracted one of the *People* people. That there may be unpleasant repercussions, sometimes, seems to astonish them.

Zsa Zsa's explanation of her fling with Rubirosa

is fairly baroque but not altogether implausible. Evidently, she and Sanders were at a party at Ciro's when Doris Duke came up to her husband, kissed him on both cheeks, and said, "Darling, didn't we have fun this afternoon?"

Sanders' explanation was that they had the same voice teacher and that on occasion, that day being one of those, they had a drink together.

Zsa Zsa was suspicious enough, however, to hire a private detective, who soon reported that he had tracked Sanders and Ms. Duke to a motel. Her chagrin and anger were enough to prompt her to what can only be described as a calculated act of revenge sex—she'd get even with them by having an affair with Rubirosa, to whom Doris Duke had been married and whom she still loved and wanted to remarry.

How novelistic of her! Or it is the setup for a bedroom farce with many doors and windows through which, in the third act, people will be making entrances and exits, just missing one another, hiding under furniture, overhearing snatches of conversations, the meanings of which they are getting wrong, and making us laugh just enough to suppress our discomfort.

There were, apparently, other stresses in her marriage to Sanders. He was not altogether comfortable with the success she was enjoying as a movie actress—although in retrospect the career seems mostly laughable. It was at about this time that she made *We're Not Married!*, an anthology film about five couples who discover that, because of an administrative glitch, they are not married after all. Zsa Zsa played the gold-digging bride of Louis Calhern, an older millionaire. (After her marriage to Conrad Hilton, this was no great stretch for her.)

Marilyn Monroe was in that picture, too, although she and Zsa Zsa had no scenes together.

Zsa Zsa's next film was *Moulin Rouge*, which opened in the spring of 1953 in New York. Sanders, she says, refused to attend the premiere, although it is likelier that the invitation from Roberto Rossellini for him to come to Rome to make *Viaggio in Italia (Voyage in Italy)* with Ingrid Bergman might have been the real reason for his failure to show up at this event.

At any rate, on the opening night of *Moulin Rouge*, furious with Sanders, who she thought should have been there, she met Rubirosa in the elevator of the Plaza. He sent her flowers and invited her to meet him and Prince Bernadotte in the Persian Room for a drink.

Flowers! A prince! The Persian Room!

Ah, magic! But she was angry at Sanders, remember, and it is safe to assume that she hadn't forgotten her rage at Doris Duke.

So she accepts and goes to meet him there, but she takes her mother with her.

As protection? As cover? As agent?

★

I used to go to the Persian Room. A lot. *Newsweek* didn't have a show business section, so nightclub singers, when we wrote about them, had to be put in the music department. And Emily Coleman thought it was beneath her dignity to do nightclubs. It was also demanding in that one had to stay up quite late, which she didn't like to do. So before I got the movie desk and was a back-of-the-book "swinger," I'd go to Basin Street East or the Copa or the Persian Room, and while it was glamorous enough, it was also aggressively frivolous.

It was after coming home one morning from the Persian Room that I first asked myself if this was what I wanted to do with my life. And as with questions about whether or not you need a haircut, if you're asking, you already know the answer.

"Mother and I went to the Persian Room, and it was then that I met him. It was then that Rubi finally impressed me. He was dark, magnetic, as mysterious in his own way as Atatürk had been in his, as cool and composed as Conrad Hilton, and as sophisticated and urbane as George Sanders. Before we ever even touched, Rubi mesmerized me."

What nonsense. She wanted to get back at Sanders and Duke for their infidelity or, to be more accurate, his affront to her amour propre, which was far stronger than her amour for anyone or anything else.

But then, as I remember it, the Persian Room itself was nonsense, with those waiters dressed up in their ridiculous Persian costumes.

Still, they did a really good steak tartare.

As Zsa Zsa tells it, she and Rubi spent "one night together at the Plaza," and in the morning she knew she never wanted to leave him again.

Presumably it was that same night. And one wonders, what did she say to her mother?

He was "exciting, sensual, passionate, primitive yet incredibly sophisticated."

But she and her cowriter are perhaps spicing this up for the readers. If we are using her experience for our fantasies, vicariously delighting in her extravagances, we want him to have been wonderful. And given the machinery of the setup in which he is demonstrating that he is not tied to Doris Duke and her millions and she is showing that she can be as much an adventurer as George Sanders, he could have been quite ordinary and yet managed to serve his purpose. Sex is in large measure a fantasy for real people; for fantasy people—and this is what they are, what they do, how they make a living, and how they live—there isn't a whole lot of external reality to conform to or appeal to.

The relationship between Sanders and Zsa Zsa

was complicated, but one would expect that. When Zsa Zsa was on Broadway in *Forty Carats* in 1969, Sanders came to the theater every night. He'd had the first of a series of slight strokes and was recovering, but managed to say to her clearly enough, "You're the big star, and I just sit backstage and wait for you." He watched her, of course, thinking now and again of *A Star Is Born* with its hammy chiasmus. But he could still make suggestions. He took her costar, Michael Nouri, aside and told him he wasn't kissing Zsa Zsa hard enough. The next night, Nouri kissed her hard enough to tear her dress, and Sanders, she reports, "was elated. The fire rekindled." They were, at this point, divorced, and Sanders floated the idea that they might remarry. "But I followed the advice of friends like Pamela Mason and refused," Zsa Zsa reports.

In her other autobiography (two? why not?), the one "written for me by Gerold Frank," she explains her meeting with Rubi by saying, "And I was drunk that moment—drunk with power, drunk with achievement, drunk with yearning for George. I was in a daze—and overexcited, so overhappy, so overemotional, so overmiserable because George was not there for my moment of triumph, because George had said, 'No, don't come to Rome, you'll spoil my fun,' because here was Rubirosa, the most pursued of men, the only man whose name could make George grow pale—because I was overexcited and overmiserable and overlonely and overeverything, I said yes."

I think of Delmore Schwartz's famous poem, "In the Naked Bed, in Plato's Cave," and I realize that in that bed is . . . Zsa Zsa!

So now she is like a suicide bomber, the fact of her infidelity a weapon strapped to her body that she can use at any time. And even if she doesn't use it, the knowledge that she can is empowering and exhilarating.

Except that she is a creature of impulse, given to melodramatic posturings, self-indulgent, all but delusional, and at least for the time being, lulled by an indulgent world that gives her reason to believe her fantasies are not absolutely unreal. How much hope is there for her to restrain herself, not tell George, not, at some opportune moment, fling it in his face?

Looking back on her life, she talks in her book about her acting career and says that if she had concentrated on that her life might have been completely different.

She appeared in films, but she was no more an actress than Flipper or Lassie or Rin Tin Tin.

Again, in a mildly surprising way, Zsa Zsa gets some credit for not blurting it out. She was able, at least for a little while, to keep her secret. And she joined Sanders in Rome, where he was making

Viaggio in Italia. Astonishingly, Gabor disapproved of Ingrid Bergman, Sanders' costar, for having left Petter Lindström for Rossellini. She quotes her friend André de Toth as saying, "There was hardly an electrician on the set that she [Bergman] didn't sleep with. When she was finished with them, she had them fired."

But she reveals that the reason for her dislike of Bergman was a lack of proper deference. The day they arrived, she says, "Ingrid, noticing me, sailed over and said, 'Oh, I want to meet George's wife.' Given my burgeoning career, it felt like a slap, so I replied, 'And I'd like to meet Roberto's wife.'"

Sanders hated the picture, didn't understand what Rossellini was doing, couldn't adapt and improvise. It is the only art film he ever made, a milestone of the cinema, actually, and an important precursor to the work of Antonioni. But Sanders didn't get it.

That can happen with actors. They're not too smart, some of them. I remember hearing that nobody on the set of John Huston's *Beat the Devil,* one of my favorite movies, ever let Jennifer Jones know that what they were making was a comedy. She played it absolutely straight and was wonderful doing so. Only after the film came out did she learn that everyone but her had been in on the joke, and even though people thought the film was marvelous, she was furious and felt betrayed.

★

Zsa Zsa kept quiet about her fling with Rubi, but Sanders found out anyway, because Rubirosa sent a romantic telegram to her in Rome, which Sanders found. (Did he open it? Had she left it lying around? Are there, as Freud suggests, no accidents after all?)

A crucial scene, but how do they play it? Has anyone told them that it's a comedy? And are they smart enough to know that comedy is also serious? Movie stars though they are, they are vulnerable to the same vicissitudes that affect the rest of us. Indeed, their fluctuations between wealth and need, fame and obscurity, and, for that matter, happiness and misery are greater than those of the rest of us, the mere spectators.

Sanders is jealous, perhaps, but jealousy is not always a bad thing. It can be spicy. Zsa Zsa describes an assignation she made at Sanders' urging with a priest they had met on the train. It amused Sanders to think of her balling the priest, and he enjoyed the wickedness of it. She claims that when she discovered that the priest was actually a virgin, she changed her mind and, in the end, did not have sex with him—but she didn't tell Sanders this and let him imagine her performing the entire manual of arms with the padre. And this was exciting enough to rouse him from the depression into which he had been plunged by Rossellini's quirky moviemaking.

Let us assume that he felt . . . annoyance, not at the infidelity but the betrayal, the public nature of this. Rubirosa, that notorious coxman and lounge lizard? If she just wanted to fuck someone, why couldn't she avail herself of one of Ingrid Bergman's cast-off electricians? But to go off to Paris to frolic with Rubi would be to humiliate him and make him a laughingstock. Couldn't she see that? Didn't she care about him? Weren't they, in some vague way, allies? Shouldn't they be thinking of each other at least a little? Isn't this what married people do?

The big question that each of us has to answer is whether other people are real. Mostly, this is not difficult, at least not for those who have passed their fourth birthday. This is what preschool is mostly about. But movie actors unlearn these lessons and entertain doubts not only about the existence of other people but even about their own. Zsa Zsa must have risked wrinkling her forehead as she thought about what Sanders was saying—sneering? Or, just a little out of character, even raising his voice?

What decided it for her was the other invitation to come to Paris to begin shooting on *The Most Wanted Man* with Fernandel. This way, it wasn't just Rubirosa, who might or might not be a passing fancy, but her career, which was, she thought, her continuing and legitimate passion. And Sanders had no right to stand in her way!

But still, no final rupture, which suggests that he did care for her. He hoped that it might perhaps go away. He continued the work he hated on *Viaggio in Italia*. And then when that was a wrap, flew up to Cannes, where he found her with Rubirosa. Rubi was there with Zsa Zsa but was courting Barbara Hutton. And they all had lunch with the Aga Khan!

Names, names, names. With such names as these, the verbs don't count, do they?

But they do. Zsa Zsa flew back to Paris with Rubi. Sanders flew to New York, where Jolie Gabor, Zsa Zsa's mother, refused to take any of this seriously and told him that her daughter was only doing this "*pour passer le temps.*" He flew on to Los Angeles, went to the Bel Air house, unpacked, had a swim in the pool, and then began looking for a house to rent so that he could move the fuck out.

4

THE ROSSELLINI MOVIE MAY NOT

be great, but it is extraordinary and very important in what it enabled for other moviemakers. As Andrew Sarris remarked, it is "one of the most influential films in modern cinema, strongly affecting the works of Resnais, Antonioni, Fellini, and the entire New Wave." Sanders was doing it partly as a favor to Ingrid Bergman, with whom he had worked years before on *Rage in Heaven*.

Bergman's and Sanders' characters arrive in Naples, where one of them—it is never quite clear which—has inherited a villa from an Uncle Homer. They are taking advantage of this business transaction to get away together, which they seem never to have done before. Their marriage, we see at once, is on very shaky ground.

As was Bergman's to Rossellini. And Sanders' to Gabor.

For the first time, and perhaps the only time in all his movies, Sanders' mannerisms, his affected elocution, his sneer, and his elegant address are turned inside out and shown to be defensive, or at least distancing, gestures. In *All About Eve,* he delivers a zinger and that's it, the camera cuts away, and he is like a tennis player who has served an ace. Here the camera lingers for a while longer, and we see the hurt on Bergman's face, and then the recognition, on Sanders' part, that what he has said was unkind and unwarranted, and then his wavering—should he take it back, apologize, try somehow to mollify? In other words, he descends from the fantasy plane of most of his movies to real life, where these mannerisms are as clumsy and as difficult to maneuver as the behemoth Bentley they drive through the streets of Naples. It is a grand automobile, and Rossellini spends a lot of time showing it stopped by herds of cattle, swarms of people, religious processions, and the other intrusions of real life on its pretensions of luxury and size.

I had a Rolls once, for a few days anyway. Another classmate of mine needed to sell some stuff, I think to take care of his mother who was unwell. He offered it to me at a good price, and I could not resist. It was a 1948 Silver Wraith sports saloon, and it had cut crystal vases for flowers in the backseat, and the owner's manual was leather bound and in a slipcase.

Its first sentence began, "For optimal performance of your automobile, instruct your driver as to the following . . . ." It was lovely but very heavy and almost impossible to steer. My wife couldn't get it out of the driveway. So I had to return it and let him sell it to someone else for more money than I'd paid for it. But for that week, I was an aristocrat, a grandee, a movie star!

It is a painful movie to watch, knowing what we know about these people and, in particular, hearing the resonances of Sanders' suicide note in so much of the dialogue. They keep discussing boredom. In a line in the first scene of the film, Sanders remarks, "What noisy people! I've never seen noise and boredom go so well together." Bergman replies, "I don't know, Uncle Homer lived here for forty years without getting bored." And Sanders answers, "Uncle Homer was not a normal person."

Which leaves us, of course, with the question as to whether these are "normal" people. In Naples, the aggressively foreign Bergman and Sanders are cut off from the sources of religion, history, and folk culture that make Italian life so vibrant. Their anomie is as much a manifestation of their sophistication as their fine car, their elegant clothing, and their separate, if connecting, rooms at the Excelsior.

"I'm just bored because I've nothing to do," Sanders says. And it is a subject to which they return often.

What can they do to save their marriage and themselves? What comes to mind? When he asks, "Shall we have something to drink?" she says, "Yes, but not here. Let's go down to the bar. At least there'll be some other people around."

"Why?" he asks, making what is a very diffident advance. "Would it be so terribly boring if we were to remain alone?"

"No," she says, "I was thinking of you. I don't think you're very happy when we're alone."

"Are you sure you know when I'm happy?" he asks with a condescending smile that may not even be habitual. It is either his character's habitual manner or, certainly, Sanders' habitual performance mode.

She tells him, in words that are not necessarily a complaint or an attack, that they are like strangers. He puts the best light he can manage on that observation by suggesting that, "Now that we're strangers, we can start all over again at the beginning. It might be rather amusing, don't you think?"

She considers this for a fraction of a second and says, "Let's go down to the bar."

The terms of their discussion, of their marriage, and, indeed, of their lives are set out for us: boring or amusing. And it is clearly Rossellini's purpose not to satirize them, or at least not them alone, but to make an indictment of modern life, for clearly these are not adequate categories with which to confront our joys and sorrows. And Sanders' suicide note with its complaint about boredom is now, for those of us who are paying the right kind of attention, a part of the film.

That Sanders couldn't understand what was going on, objected to Rossellini's lackadaisical methods of filmmaking, and generally hated the experience is irrelevant. Rossellini was perhaps amused, but eventually bored, by Sanders' continual complaining. As he said in an interview he gave to *Filmcritica* in the spring of 1965, "He moaned terribly, and I used to say to him, 'What are you getting so depressed about? At the worst, you'll have made one more bad film—nothing worse than that can happen. I don't see anything to cry about in that. There's no cause for despair. We've all made good films and bad films. So we'll make another bad one. What can you do? There's no need to tear your hair out or kill yourself over it.'"

And then he explains that he used Sanders' unhappiness. "You can use anything, even an actor's temper. You see something in a moment of temper, a certain expression or attitude that you can use, and so of course, you use it."

The interviewers ask Rossellini, "Why did you choose Sanders?"

"Don't you think he was obvious for the part?" Rossellini asks back. "It was his bad moods rather than his own personality that suited the character in the film."

But as we come to learn, bad moods were his personality.

He was so desperate that he threatened to walk away from the picture. To placate him and to help him get through the ordeal—Sanders, Rossellini knew, was talking by telephone every night to his psychiatrist in New York—the director acceded to his request that Zsa Zsa join them in Naples. That this would do little to improve Sanders' spirits, Rossellini could not have known. Almost certainly, he was trying to help. After all, the terms of his deal with the financial backers were that their supplying the money was contingent on Sanders' being a part of the film. He may have revealed this to Sanders in an effort to shame him into behaving honorably and professionally. At any rate, on-screen we can see that look of torment on Sanders' face and read in his body posture a discomfort that is not feigned. Or, if it is, then beneath the mask of suffering is real suffering, which gives it a certain authority.

It is a slight film in terms of narrative. They arrive in Naples. Katherine Joyce (Bergman) goes to see the sights—the National Archaeological Museum, Cumae, the Phlegraean Fields where smoke and steam come rising out of the earth, the Fontanelle Cemetery, and then, with Alex (Sanders), Pompeii. Alex, meanwhile, takes off for Capri in search of "fun," which is to say that he has a flirtation with a young woman in which he fails to score. And he has another near miss with a prostitute back in Naples who is too unutterably sad to have sex with. The husband and wife bicker, make feeble attempts to connect but are out of synch in these efforts, and Alex, almost on a whim, suggests a divorce, to which Katherine, with some dismay, agrees. Then, as they are leaving Naples, their Bentley gets caught up in a religious procession in a small town on the Amalfi coast. The huge car can't move. They get out, and Katherine is carried away by the surging crowd that is shouting, "*Miracolo! Miracolo!*" Alex manages to rescue her, and in their relief now that the moment of panic has passed, they embrace. And there is a kind of reconciliation.

Alexander: Katherine, what's wrong with us? Why do we torture each other?

Katherine: When you say things that hurt me, I try to hurt you back, don't you see? But I can't any longer, because I love you.

Alexander: Perhaps we get hurt too easily.

Katherine: Tell me that you love me.

Alexander: Well, if I do, will you promise not to take advantage of me?

Katherine: Oh, yes, but I want to hear you say it.

Alexander: All right, I love you.

It is either a happy ending or else a momentary thing that cannot last, an ironic and sad indication of the miracle that could have been the ending if either of these northern sophisticates actually believed in miracles.

It is at once simple and straightforward and also complicated and layered. In one of their quarrels, Katherine quotes the poetry of Charles Lewington, a poet, now dead, with whom she had some sort of relationship before she met Alex. Alex is jealous and dismissive. There are critics who see in this an echo of James Joyce's "The Dead," in which Gretta speaks of Michael Furey, the singer, and arouses her husband's jealousy. (This perhaps explains why Alex's surname is Joyce.) Rossellini was, himself, jealous of Robert Capa, the photographer, with whom Bergman had had an affair before they met and who was still alive. (He died in 1954, in Indochina, where he was killed by a land mine.) The Capri excursion is, geographically, a bit awkward, but Capri was for many years the home of one of Rossellini's mistresses, Roswitha Schmidt, a German nightclub dancer. Among his other mistresses were Marcella de Marchis, his former wife; Marilyn Buferd, who was Miss America 1946; and Anna Magnani—the cat lady.

All of this is relevant. Everything is relevant in movies. It is a messy business and a messy art. The people at *Time* were wrong to have a show business section and a cinema section, as if to keep the business and the gossip separate from the artistic results. One could tell a lot about a movie just from knowing the budget. Too small and there would be too few interiors and a lot of cutting of corners, and the constraints would hurt it; too large and there would be cowardly and vulgar decisions forced on the producer, the writer, and the director, to attract and hold the huge audience that was required to recoup such sums. At *Newsweek* we just had a movies department, which was less pretentious and in which it was acknowledged that any part of it, from money to gossip, can be of interest.

Viaggio in Italia was never widely released and made no money. And the critics mostly hated it. Or, I should say, the reviewers. Critics later on realized that it was an important, innovative, and in many ways, admirable film. Or at least some of them did. But the reviewers?

There is an interesting suggestion in Peter Bondanella's book *The Films of Roberto Rossellini* (Cambridge University Press, 1993) that the Italian reviewers hated it because they were still shocked and angry about Rossellini's notorious affair with Ingrid Bergman. Italy's conservative and mostly Catholic critics came down on it, therefore, with particular venom. (One wrote, "*Viaggio in Italia* is more than an ugly film. It is a true and proper insult to the intelligence of the audience.") The French, meanwhile, who ought to have come to the defense of both Rossellini and the movie, were angry at him because they were mostly leftists, and Rossellini seemed to have turned away from social protest and ideology and was indulging himself with introspective cinema.

And the Americans? Those few who did see it had no idea what they were looking at.

Only when I was reviewing movies did I come to understand what a bunch of dopes my colleagues were. They didn't know anything about art or literature or culture—which would have disqualified them, actually, as representatives of the public. I could get any movie a bad notice in the *New York Times* simply by coming early to the screening room, sitting in the seat next to the one Bosley Crowther liked, and putting my Danish pastry or my sandwich on what he thought of as his seat. This was an affront to a person who was my parents' age and who, because he was at the *Times,* considered himself to be the dean of American film reviewers.

I tried the experiment maybe three times. It always worked. After that, I stopped because it was no longer amusing and because I was costing the distributors of the films we'd been watching millions of dollars.

Naughty of me? I suppose. And irresponsible. On the other hand, it doesn't speak well for Crowther's sense of responsibility either. Or, now that I think of it, for Sanders'. He got back to Hollywood in what was, we may agree, a foul mood, but it was above and beyond the call of mischievousness to bad-mouth the picture he had just made with Rossellini and tell everyone he could what a turkey it was, hoping it would never get picked up and distributed.

That neither he nor Bergman had any idea of the excellence of the work that Rossellini was doing is regrettable, but then movie actors are not exactly intellectuals. Bergman never liked *Casablanca* either, couldn't figure out what her character was supposed to be doing in most of the scenes and rather resented the film's awards and its elevation to greatness. I rather doubt that either Sanders or Bergman had even read "The Dead."

This is the movie about which Jacques Rivette wrote in *Cahiers du Cinéma,* "If there is a modern cinema, this is it," and "with the appearance of *Viaggio in Italia,* all films have suddenly aged ten years." In Bernardo Bertolucci's first movie, *Prima della rivoluzione,* one of his characters is a cineaste who has seen *Viaggio in Italia* fifteen times and who says, "Remember, you cannot live without Rossellini."

Without question, it is the most interesting and most important film Sanders ever made. He was a supporting player in *All About Eve.* Here, he was the lead, and he wasn't playing his usual caricature scoundrel, cad, or pimp in a good suit. "*Miracolo! Miracolo!*" the simple people in the streets of Maiori cry out in the procession of the Madonna at the end of *Viaggio in Italia,* and it appears that a blind man has regained his sight. But Alex and Katherine, sophisticated northerners whose souls have atrophied and whose minds have been corrupted by modern life, can't accept it. It is they who cannot see. "How can they believe in that? They're like a bunch of children," Alex complains. (Sanders and Bergman, the actors, couldn't believe in the miraculous film either.)

Their reconciliation satisfies the conventions of commercial filmmaking, and it, too, is a "miracle," but it doesn't require a lot of cerebration to figure that miracles are lost on those who are blind to them and that the reconciliation is unlikely to last.

There is one more short shot with which the film concludes—of an impassive member of the marching band who is on the scene, supposedly for crowd control, although, clearly, he hasn't been doing a very good job. For those inclined to think in such terms, he may represent a distanced god who, even if he knows everything and understands everything, no longer exerts himself to interfere.

5

THERE WAS AN IDEA THAT WAS

floated around the office back in my *Newsweek* days that maybe the critical pieces—on books, theater, music, movies, and art—should be signed. I resisted it, because I was willing to sign the checks they issued (smallish, I'm afraid) but not copy that they had fiddled with. I had grandiose ideas of my auteur status as an author. I also happened to be the unit chairman of the Newspaper Guild, so the editors backed down and figured, sensibly, that I might not be there forever. Or that if I stayed on for long enough, I'd grow up.

But I was wrong. The relation between a reader and a movie reviewer is curious, but personal. There isn't any objective standard by which to judge movies. There is only the impact that a film has on a personality and sensorium that the reader gets to know and, perhaps, trust. The movie reviewer

I most cared about back when I was doing it was Brendan Gill, over at the *New Yorker,* who brought a bemused sophistication to whatever he encountered. This wasn't without its costs, I am afraid. He had been (and the pluperfect can be a very cruel tense) an interesting and lively writer of fiction (*Ways of Loving* and *The Day the Money Stopped*). But then there came a day when the fiction stopped, and he ... gave up, I guess. Still, he was dapper, a kind of old Yalie I admired—urban, urbane, and wonderfully poised—and, in some sense, wanted to be like when I grew up.

He had come up to Yale to talk to us under-graduates—it must have been in 1954 or so—to tell us how to be writers. Not how to write, but how to be writers. And he said that there were two rules. One, sponge off your parents for as long as humanly possible, and then, two, marry money. It was a little like Harold Clurman's sad line about how there is a life in the theater but not, alas, a living. But it had an insouciance that made it memorable.

Even if one disagreed with Gill about a film, there were pleasures in reading his reviews. Being right, after all, is hardly the point. What counts is to be interesting and, in some way or another, appealing. Reviewers can't hurt a big movie. The studios spend as much advertising and distributing a film, sometimes, as they spend on the film itself. And many of the movies make the bulk of their money the first week, or even the first weekend, that they hit the screens. Back in my day, what I could do was help a little film, like *Ride the High Country,* a gem of a decadent western, an early Sam Peckinpah movie with Randolph Scott and Joel McCrea that opened on the bottom of a double bill. *Newsweek*'s clout could rescue it from the obscurity to which the studio executives had consigned it. It won, I think, some Belgian film award (The Golden Sprout?) and has become a cult classic. We could also take a small European movie and help it. But big studio behemoths were, and are, invulnerable.

In a strange way, what made Gill and me, too, I think, interesting reviewers is that, for quite different reasons, we didn't care. I can't really speak for him except insofar as this is the impression I had from reading his reviews. I know that in my case, *Newsweek* was something one did in the daytime to make money. My real life was elsewhere. Like Trollope, I would get up very early, go to my study, write for an hour or so, and then dress and go to work. And on the train into New York (I'd see Bosley Crowther standing on the platform, but I went into the smoking car and he didn't), I studied my copy of Clyde Pharr's *Homeric Greek.* This was serious. The appointment we both had, at ten thirty, to go to a screening room and see a new Annette Funicello movie was, obviously, not serious. I found it fascinating that at his age—my parents' age—he could still do this. I thought it was brave of him. Or cowardly, maybe. But surely weird.

I couldn't imagine myself in thirty years still doing this. (Even if I had stayed at the desk, it would have been, after three decades, a different self.)

In an essentially pointless and frivolous undertaking, earnestness is not helpful or even relevant. My readers, whom I could barely imagine, weren't interested in the art of the film or being educated about it. All they wanted was an entertaining voice that might also tell them whether a movie might be worth going to see. Ebert and Roeper have refined that down to an imperial thumbs-up or thumbs-down. But surely that isn't interesting.

Literary criticism can be, at least sometimes, inherently interesting and serious. A very few writers about movies have managed to make valuable observations, Robert Warshow most notably. But some of the famous ones are famous for peculiar reasons. People talk about how observant James Agee was when he had the cinema desk at *Time,* and he could, indeed, see what was in front of him. But he could also miss stuff. One of his famous reviews is of *Meet Me in St. Louis* with Judy Garland, and he does a lyrical paragraph about the rich sepia tones of the film and how that is the color of nostalgia. It is also the color of an out-of-register print, which was what he happened to be shown. Look at it on DVD in the colors that the director and cinematographer had in mind, and you wonder what the hell he was talking about.

I sat at the desk for a couple of years and learned a lot. About movies and about life, too, I have to admit. I discovered that the most frivolous approach to movies one could manage was still far too serious. The people who make movies are absolutely ignorant about a) what's any good and b) what's likely to sell. They are like a convention of astrologers, each of whom knows that what he's doing is pure bullshit but still can take comfort in the fact that, if there are so many of them here in the same place, maybe there's something to it after all.

I know, for instance, how *Sex and the Single Girl* got made, and it's all true and all too silly for Nathanael West to have tried to write.

It begins with Martin Goldblatt, a decent fellow, smart enough but not too smart, who is the publicist for Richard Quine, the director. The nub of the story is that Quine has back taxes to pay and alimony and child support, and who knows what else, and while he's living high on the hog with those velvet slippers embroidered with a *Q* in a circle all done in real gold thread, he doesn't have money to throw away on nonessentials like, for instance, paying Goldblatt. For a year and a half!

Goldblatt's idea is that he'll go to New York and get himself a real job or, at any rate, a job that pays in negotiable checks. But to get from Los Angeles to New York City, you can't walk. You're not going to take a goddamned bus! You fly! And this means you need to borrow a few bucks for the plane ticket. And a couple of days in a not too expensive hotel, like the Shoreham maybe, which is across the street from William Morris (or it was then) and is pleasantly beat-up, a kind of East Coast Chateau Marmont. Say, five hundred dollars? But who will lend you such a sum?

Goldblatt decides that the one he'll put the bite on will be Tony Curtis, with whom he'd been friendly in Paris the year before when he'd been over there with Quine as they did a movie for George Axelrod called *Paris—When It Sizzles.* Curtis had done Axelrod a favor by showing up to do some work on the movie when William Holden had to be shipped off to a clinic to dry out. And then, only a few days later, Holden crashed his Ferrari into a wall and had his arm in a cast.

Holden liked the Shoreham. It was where he fell over, drunk, hit his head either on a table or a radiator, and died. It was a drunk's death, sad but not actually surprising to him or to anyone else. But at least he didn't have to do anything in particular to bring it about. Sanders might have envied that. For Holden, it came as a kind of gift.

I used to stay there because Holden died there, but they've tarted the place up now and made it aggressively nouveau and also aggressively expensive, so I don't anymore. And William Morris has moved, and anyway, they are no longer my agents. But when I walk by the place I think of him. Another stylish wreck.

Paris—When It Sizzles is not terrible. The gimmick is that Holden is a drunken screenwriter who is supposed to deliver a script to a producer, but he's been having a good time, partying, and now, just a few days before the deadline, he hires a secretary (Hepburn) to help him. Holden could put on spectacles and look like an intellectual—think of *Born Yesterday* or this film. He had that tweedy air. Hepburn is part secretary, part muse, part cowriter, and just lovely. They've got to do the whole 138-page screenplay in forty-eight hours. There are moments of real whimsy and a few fun bit parts, some credited (like Noël Coward, who plays the producer) and others not (like Mel Ferrer, Hepburn's husband at the time). Marlene Dietrich shows up for a couple of minutes and gets out of a white Rolls. ("Or, no, make it a Bentley," Holden says as the screenwriter. "That's got more class.") So she gets out of the Rolls, but that turns instantly into a Bentley, and she walks into Dior's. That's it. It must have taken an hour of her time to do.

Curtis does an almost funny bit playing a method actor who stands Audrey Hepburn up for their Bastille Day date. And, and, and . . . they all finish the film, more or less. It's watchable, as any movie with Holden and Hepburn is likely to be if it isn't wholly stupid, although the picture is too constrained, and it spends too much time in the room, but that's what writers do. They are in a room, writing, or in this case, dictating.

What I particularly remember about it is that there was a screen credit to Hubert de Givenchy for Miss Hepburn's clothes *and perfume.* Had the movie been in Aromarama (there was such a process, no kidding), that might have made sense. But the only possible explanation is that Hepburn wanted a gallon or so of some scent he did, and Axelrod could get it inexpensively if he gave Givenchy a credit. So, done and done. But what creativity!

Modest charm, though, isn't what studio movies are about. It cost four million dollars and grossed two million dollars the first year. Floppo in Chi. Barfo in Cleve. The film was a stinker and not all the Givenchy you squirted on it would help that. Quine had made a few decent pictures, *The World of Suzie Wong, Strangers When We Meet,* and *Bell Book and Candle,* but understandably, the studios' interest in him was now rather diminished. And Goldblatt's prospects were therefore dim indeed.

You don't want to do this too formally. It's better if it's a by-the-way, offhand thing. And Goldblatt knows that Curtis' favorite pastime is to go out to the garage and polish the body work of his Rolls-Royces and Bentleys. With real chamois from Yugoslavia, yet. Goldblatt calls and asks if Tony would like company doing this. A writer would have figured out a more plausible approach, but this worked. Sure, come on over, Curtis said, unable to imagine anyone who wouldn't like washing cars on a Sunday afternoon.

Goldblatt goes over to Curtis' place, grabs a chamois, and starts polishing. Why not? It's cleaning up, it's making nice, it's what publicists do anyway. And on maybe the second hood, he mentions that he is broke, hoping to go to New York and find a job, and needs some money. Curtis is hurt. That Goldblatt had some ulterior motive and wasn't here for the love of the cars? A sad thought. Also, Curtis doesn't like to lend money, because as he explains, it ruins friendships. Goldblatt is flattered that Curtis is declaring their friendship to be important to him, but that doesn't get him out of Los Angeles. What then to do?

Curtis has a suggestion. He'll make a few calls. And right there, in the garage, with Goldblatt polishing and rubbing, Curtis calls a few friends. Hank Fonda, Betty Bacall, Natalie Wood, and Mel Ferrer, and in each case, the pitch is the same—that it would be fun to make a movie, and would they be in it with him, and would it be okay if Richard Quine directs? See, the scheme is that if Curtis can put together an actual movie, there on the spot, and get Quine hired, then Quine will be able to come up with at least enough of Goldblatt's back pay to let him buy his ticket—if that's what he still wants to do.

The movie is *Sex and the Single Girl,* whichWarner Brothers had bought for eight hundred thousand dollars. It was a big joke in Hollywood because they hadn't bothered to look at the book, didn't realize it was nonfiction, and had paid more than a hundred thousand dollars a word for the title, which was the only useful part. A couple of desperate screenwriters had taken a look at it, had perhaps even typed some pages, but the project, absurd and impossible on its face, had gotten nowhere and was now on the shelf.

Curtis knew that, of course, but he saw it as an opportunity. He took maybe half an hour to put together a package that a William Morris agent, working day and night, would have spent a year to put together. Curtis then calls Quine, tells him who he's lined up, and asks if Richard will consider directing. It's like asking a street beggar if he will consider a ten dollar bill. Quine is not difficult to persuade.

It'll all work out, he promises Goldblatt, who has been in the business long enough not to be surprised by much, but this is . . . ridiculous!

It is, of course, but it is also a symptom of what happens when the old studio system collapses. Individual producers, now out on their own, are putting together packages that depend on the bankability of their stars, because it's a matter now of adding up what the banks think they can rely on each one of them bringing in. Curtis is no fool and understands this. Add up Fonda, Bacall, Wood, Ferrer, and himself, and you've got a movie. Despite Quine.

The whole project is a lark, so he gets Quine to ask for Joseph Heller as the writer. Heller's *Catch-22* has just been published and has had great success. Heller can be funny. (He doesn't need any money, the tax rate back then being something like 70 percent, but he'll do it for the last word in drop-dead hi-fi and for lodging in one of the bungalows of the Beverly Hills Hotel during the entire project—all of which costs a lot but is still less than what they'd have to pay him in cash.)

Reviewing it in the *New York Times,* Abe Weiler said, "It's not the worst picture ever made, girls and boys. No kidding." This was an in-joke, because a number of people in the business knew how the thing had been put together. Heller and his cowriter, David Schwartz (somebody had to know something about the construction of a script), have some really funny bits, such as the scene in the zoo where Curtis, as the sleazo tabloid writer, and Wood, as Helen Gurley Brown, do a kind of rowdy love scene-cum-argument, and the monkeys in their cages watch with skepticism and disapproval. Fonda and Bacall almost steal the picture, and Quine does what he always did, with madcap Keystone Cops chases.

But none of it is as funny as the idea that Mr. Curtis was trying to find some solution to

Goldblatt's problem other than lending him a few hundred dollars.

Some years later, Goldblatt gave me a car, or more accurately, asked me to take it off his hands. He'd won it in a card game either from a Princess d'Arenberg or perhaps from her chauffeur. It was a huge Lincoln Premier convertible, bright red, and it had only been used to convey the princess's salukis from Newport down to Palm Beach and back. Its cream leather seats were spotted with saluki drool, but it was otherwise in fine shape. The trouble with it was that Goldblatt didn't drive, didn't even have a license, and was paying more than he could afford to garage it in Manhattan. So I bought him a nice dinner and accepted it with pleasure.

It was a flashy car—so much so that I got stopped in Rhode Island once by a state trooper who assumed, not unreasonably, that anyone driving such a vehicle had to be operating on the wrong side of the law.

And my point is? That this is altogether irrational. That causes and effects have nothing to do with each other. Intentions and results are from some other universe. At a certain minimal level, any movie is interesting. There are people and animals moving. There is a guy who drives up in a car and gets out and slams the door. We see and hear all this. He walks up the steps to the front door of a house and either rings the bell or just lets himself in. We're seeing all this with our own eyes, and we have a belief in what we're witnessing that takes any novelist a good deal of fuss and trouble to achieve. It's only when the actors open their mouths and start saying stuff that the movie may lose us.

But what a hell of an advantage to have. And that's why going into a movie theater and sitting there in the semidarkness waiting for the trailers and then the feature film has a different kind of promise than what we experience opening a nice new book, even with that lovely smell of the fresh ink on the paper.

The only thing wrong with movies is that they are all seductive in this way and that audiences, and more particularly critics, tend to take them seriously. But I came to the experience as a poet who was slumming, open to amusement, and able to see and think, and therefore I had at least a little armor. It also helped that I was writing for a magazine that, had I not worked there, I wouldn't have read. That took a lot of the pressure off.

But I can sense the objection of some readers who wonder what a young snotty guy like that is doing in a position of such power. And the answer is that I was reviewing movies, which are inherently unserious and irrational, and my self-identification as an intellectual (Andover, Yale, all that) was a grounding, the place to stand that Archimedes wanted. Bosley had it tougher, being more reasonable and more responsible. He was trying to get it right and to be fair and objective. But that's impossible and self-defeating. He hated Antonioni's *L'Avventura*, but everyone else liked it. So he figured that maybe he'd been wrong, and next time he'd make up for it. So he liked *L'Eclisse*, which everyone else hated. (Monica Vitti eats a used sandwich?)

Not that I was infallible. I could miss things, mostly because I had had such a comfortable and protected childhood. I remember a line in Billy Wilder's *Kiss Me, Stupid* that went right by me. This was a severely undervalued movie, a really funny restoration comedy, in which Ray Walston wants to get Dean Martin to buy one of his songs. They live in Climax, Nevada, and Martin's car breaks down there on the way back to Los Angeles. Walston's great plan is that he will pimp out his wife to Martin, and Martin will then have to buy a song. The trouble is that Walston is insanely uxorious, and so he contrives to get rid of his own wife (Felicia Farr, but the role was written for Marilyn Monroe), and he hires the town whore (Kim Novak) to pretend to be his wife. They're sitting around the living room of Walston's house, and he's praising his impostor wife, saying how well she keeps house and cooks and gardens. And then he suggests to her that she take Martin out into the backyard and "show him your parsley."

The Legion of Decency objected to that line and claimed that "parsley" means "pubic hair," which I thought was absurd and funny but their condemnation still hurt the picture at the box office. As I discovered, however, the dirty old monsignor was correct, and I was mistaken. Years after I left the magazine, when I was looking up something else in a dictionary of slang, I happened to come across "parsley," to which it gave, of course, that meaning. But that didn't bother me at all. Hooray for Mr. Wilder! (My enthusiastic notice did not help it much, I'm afraid. It was released by the artsy end of United Artists, Lopert Films, and did very poorly. It was a joke in Hollywood, where they called it "Kiss It, Stupid.")

To be irresponsible, cheeky, irreverent, and to have fun was quite enough to keep me going for the couple of years I served in that department. I could have held out a little longer. But not forever. It eats you up. What it was really like, I think, was going to the movies on a Saturday night in New Haven with a whole lot of friends and classmates and calling out impertinent things to the screen—for the amusement of our cohort. I'm told that there was a guy at Princeton (I won't give his name) who used to go on Friday night so as to be equipped with zingers for the next evening when the audience was "his."

That arrogance kept me going and then let me walk away when I was turning thirty. That hardly seems like much of a milestone now, but at the time there seemed to be a clear suggestion that I should get on with my life, that I should stop renting it out and live in it myself. James Agee, who had been one of the Yale Younger Poets, spent all those years at *Time,* then quit and figured he'd now turn to writing his own things. But a month or two later, on John Huston's tennis court, he had a heart attack and dropped dead.

What's breathtaking, it seems to me, is that the quirkiness of purpose of *Sex and the Single Girl* turns out not to be so unusual. The small size of the loan that Curtis was avoiding was absurd, but there are other, grander financial motives that come into play. I remember how I was amused to learn that the point of *The Fall of the Roman Empire* was to free up blocked pesetas. It was an expensive movie, but that was the idea. If you make a flick that costs just under twenty million (a lot for 1964), and you spend it mostly in pesetas, if you get back about ten million, it would be in real money. Negotiable dollars and yen and francs and pounds sterling. In the event, it made only half that—just under five million dollars. But that's irrelevant.

There are expensive stars in it—Sophia Loren, who got a million dollars (in real money), Stephen Boyd (replacing Charlton Heston), and Christopher Plummer (replacing Richard Harris), as well as Alec Guinness, James Mason, Anthony Quayle, Omar Sharif, Mel Ferrer, and John Ireland—but you could do a contract where you paid them a little less and gave them a percentage of the profits, because there weren't any profits and nobody intended for there ever to be any. Still, it looked good, and you could appeal to greed to cheat these people, who were rich anyway, right?

There was also a score by Dimitri Tiomkin that won an Oscar for "best substantially original score" (a category vertiginous to contemplate). Perhaps most interestingly you could rent the Spanish Army. The Yugoslavian and Spanish armies were for rent for battle scenes, and most of them could actually ride horses. You couldn't use them to invade some other country (although that would be a great idea for a movie), but you could dress them up as Romans or Greeks or Venusians. Anything you wanted. And you could pay them in pesetas, which otherwise couldn't be spent on anything outside Spain except airline tickets.

It was a big showy rather boring movie, with gladiator fights and huge crowd scenes, in comparison to which *300*'s computer-generated figures look unpersuasive. But one admires it as a piece of creative accounting. Those guys with the pocket protectors are not irrelevant out there. *Cleopatra* has never made back its initial investment and still shows itself as a loss in Twentieth Century Fox's books. But Twentieth Century Fox Releasing, a wholly owned subsidiary, has made huge amounts. The usual deal is for the releasing company to charge the producing company twenty-seven percent for advertising and making prints and doing all that kind of thing. On a five million dollar movie, that works out to be roughly fair. But a ten million dollar movie doesn't cost twice as much to advertise and distribute, and a forty million dollar picture surely doesn't cost four times that figure. So the profits of that subsidiary would be monumental. (I'm using numbers that made sense in the sixties, when I kept track, but you can adjust for inflation.)

As one of those philosophers whose name I can't remember once said, "This is a business. Art is for kids."

Movies, though, are a business for kids—both in the sense that it doesn't take, or actually discourages, braininess but also in the way the people in the business can take a childlike delight in dazzle, of which there is plenty in their world. I have been thinking about Goldblatt and the story he told me of getting invited (or, actually, getting invited *along*, with Quine and with Axelrod) to dinner at the *hôtel* of the Rothschilds in Paris during the filming of *Paris—When It Sizzles*. I have no idea which branch of the family it was, but it doesn't much matter. He told me that there was a huge dining room with a table that seated twenty-four people and with drop-dead centerpieces and luxury everywhere. But Goldblatt would have been used to all that.

What blew him away were the footmen, twelve of them in livery, standing behind the chairs, one for every two guests. Goldblatt happened to be down near the baroness, and she saw that his eyes were bugging out. A considerate hostess, she wanted to put her guest at ease, so she smiled and told him, "Don't be impressed. Half of them are borrowed from our brother."

Ah, Piotr! And Vladimir!

6

THERE ARE A FEW OTHER FILMS

Sanders made that are not altogether contemptible. He was tall and handsome, he spoke well, and he could do the technical things that movie actors have to do: walk here, stop with his toes on a line on the floor (but without looking down), look at the other actor's camera eye, and deliver, in pretty much the same way, a line of dialogue three or five or fifteen times until they have a satisfactory take for the covering two-shot, the close-up, and the other actor's close-up. Mostly, they sort it all out later in the editing room. The actors can't project too much, because the camera is quite invasive, and more often than not, there is music that will be added later to tell us what to feel, if the scene is frightening or romantic or funny or tense.

Sanders' next picture was *Call Me Madam,* and it was the first movie in which he sang, which was something he could do quite well, but because he hadn't done it before, most people assumed that he'd been dubbed. He was mostly a supporting actor, playing the villain either in a natty suit (*Witness to Murder*) or in some silly costume (*King Richard and the Crusaders, Jupiter's Darling, Moonfleet, The Scarlet Coat, The King's Thief*). It couldn't have been deeply satisfying, but he was probably able to take a craftsmanly pride in doing his part at least as well as the rest of the cast and crew were doing theirs.

He did play the lead in one interesting picture, *Death of a Scoundrel*, a B+ movie he made for RKO that was released in 1956—the year I graduated from college. What makes this one particularly interesting is that it brought him back together with Zsa Zsa and also featured his brother, Tom Conway—playing the part of his character's brother. It's a small bit at the beginning of the movie, and writer/director Charles Martin figured that if Sanders had a brother who was an actor it would be natural and amusing to use him. Sanders is Clementi Sabourin, a fictional version of Serge Rubinstein, the famous swindler. He appears at his brother's house and shop somewhere in France to find that the brother, supposing him dead, has not only appropriated his money but also married his sweetheart. Enraged and embittered, the Sanders character sells his brother out, reporting him to the police as an illegal alien. The police, in exchange, give the informant a passport and enough money to book passage to

America. They also kill the brother, which is beyond what Clementi intended, and his having caused his brother's death is what drives him over the edge so that, no longer believing in goodness, he becomes a client of the Devil. It is an absurd premise, but at least for the first half of the film, there is a stylishness and rapidity so that, with Sanders' screen persona established in so many other films, it is almost plausible.

Martin was reluctant to make Sanders too villainous for us to tolerate, and there is a kind of moral waffling in the way Sabourin's swindles work out, at least the first few times, so that the suckers are not hurt but actually come out well. In one instance, Sabourin buys a Canadian oil field and fakes the discovery of oil on the property. Then, after he has sold his shares and made a lot of money, they really do find oil, and Sabourin is annoyed that he could have made even more money if he'd held onto the shares. It was dumb when it played in theaters, but it shimmers differently now for our knowledge of Sanders' stupid and reckless business ventures— as if he had assumed that Sabourin's experiences were not the invention of a calculating and manipulative scriptwriter but possible occurrences in the real world. The redeeming innocence that Martin was trying for is exactly what Sanders' biography supplies.

The film is strenuously hokey in its denouement. Sabourin brings his poor aged mother over to

America, but he is hardly motivated by love or filial piety. He is afraid of being deported to Czechoslovakia where all his money would be confiscated. He wants his mother to declare that he is the bastard son of a Swiss citizen so that he can go to that country instead. His mother is shocked by the suggestion and its insult to her. Sabourin winds up—of course—confessing to her through a closed door that he was responsible for his brother's death and pleading for her forgiveness. And she does not open the door!

It was the last time Sanders and his brother appeared together. The breach between them, occasioned by Tom Conway's drinking, had not yet happened. Zsa Zsa plays a rich widow with whom Sabourin flirts and whose money he uses to get himself started on his series of swindles of ever greater scale. It is probably not an accident that the portrait of Zsa Zsa's husband over the fireplace looks a lot like the one of Conrad Hilton that hangs in the lobbies of Hilton hotels. Yvonne De Carlo is the female lead, the young woman in love with Sabourin who becomes his secretary and who narrates the film, explaining to the police why the number of people who might have wanted to kill him is very large indeed. It is an odd performance, as if Ms. De Carlo were doing a Joan Crawford imitation, but it works well enough. As a kind of in-joke, Sanders even does a reprise of his Addison DeWitt character in *All About Eve,* when he backs a play in order to get Zsa Zsa's secretary hired as the star, in exchange for which he expects the grateful ingénue to go to bed with him. She refuses and he has her fired, but then he relents and she is a great success. (Again, the moral ambiguity!)

The shtick of the picture, then, is that, au fond, he's a good guy. Indeed, it is his decision at the end to repay his investors that actually gets him killed—by one of his associates who does not share his remorse or his generous, quixotic impulse. This is the part of the film that is difficult to take seriously. But the absurd posturings in the office scenes in which he plays mogul have a dopey authority, because Sanders believed them and apparently thought that this was how business worked.

While the City Sleeps is the other film that deserves at least a passing mention. It is out of print and difficult to find, even though it is by Fritz Lang and therefore is of interest to college courses in the history of cinema. It is one of the pictures Lang made in America that he was proud of. Like *M*, it was about a sex murderer; although Lorre's maniac had a kind of rueful appeal, while in this one, John Barrymore Jr. is feral and almost comically loathsome. It is also a little like *Citizen Kane* with its setting in the newspaper business. (The publisher is named Walter Kyne, which is almost an Australian pronunciation of "Kane.") As Lang recalled in his interviews with Peter Bogdanovich,

"There were a lot of so-called stars in it—Sanders, [Dana] Andrews, [Thomas] Mitchell, Rhonda Fleming, Ida Lupino—you know why? Because the script was written so that with good planning, each star had no more than four or five days shooting. Therefore it was possible—simply from a financial standpoint—to put many stars in it; and every part was good."

Sanders and Lang had worked together before, on *Moonfleet*, Lang's only CinemaScope picture. Lang didn't have much use for the film and resented having to work in so unnatural a medium. It was Darryl Zanuck's answer to VistaVision, which was slightly less cumbersome. Lang told Bogdanovich that there are no pictures except *The Last Supper* that are that shape, and he said, "It was very hard to show somebody standing at a table, because either you couldn't show the table, or the person had to be back too far. And you had empty spaces on both sides which you had to fill with something. When you have two people you can fill it up with walking around, taking something someplace, and so on. But when you have only one person, there's big head and right and left you have nothing."

Sensible, intelligent, but I keep thinking of the venom of Lorre's pronouncement about "that son of a bitch!"

I have never seen *Moonfleet*, but in the stills, Sanders looks a little silly in a wig, frock coat, and knee breeches. That, I think, is to his credit. If Stewart Granger looks less ridiculous, that may be because Granger looked ridiculous all the time, and we have come to expect it of him. Sanders' performance was good enough, at any rate, so that Lang used him in his next undertaking, which was *While the City Sleeps*.

The plot is more than a little silly, involving coincidences beyond what even the most inattentive and permissive audiences are likely to accept. The dialogue is both leaden and smart-alec. The chase scene in the subway is perfunctory, nowhere near as riveting as what Lang had done in *M*. Dana Andrews appears almost out of nowhere with the police who are responding to the call, but alone he pursues the mad killer down into the subway tunnels where they fight and just miss getting killed by a passing train. What happened to all the cops? Ah, as the killer tries to escape, he ascends to the street, and up there where he emerges from the manhole, they are waiting for him!

It's incoherent and, worse, unexciting. And the sudden transformation of Walter Kyne (Vincent Price) from self-indulgent fool to sensible and decisive executive doesn't even happen on-screen but is reported to us in the last scene as Dana Andrews and his new bride read about it in the paper on their honeymoon.

Still, Sanders' performance is workmanlike, and he is nicely tailored and manipulative as he pimps Ida Lupino out to Andrews for some strategic advantage that is never made altogether clear. The picture isn't very good and is valued, I think, only because it is so hard to get hold of and is by Lang. Still, Sanders' performance in it is not disappointing.

Sanders' villainy was leavened by those delicate looks of his and his catlike grace. He walked well. (In that way, he was a little like George Raft.) He was large and therefore masculine but almost too pretty. And it was perhaps his lack of seriousness that came across to us as the next best thing to innocence. These contradictions worked for him to soften just a little what would otherwise have been too tough and therefore less interesting, if not downright unattractive.

It is not something we talk about, but it is true that some movies, some scenes in movies, are so vivid as to claim space in our souls. In Woody Allen's *Play It Again, Sam,* Allan Felix's nebbish character is made funnier by the dissonance between what we see of his behavior on-screen and what we know about his fantasies of a very different self that are informed by Humphrey Bogart's Rick in *Casablanca.* That kind of incorporation is not just a kid's diversion, an indulgence we all remember as we come out of the matinee into the unwelcome glare of daylight, but a serious aftereffect of many of our encounters with art. Painting, poetry, and sculpture teach us how to see and to be and change us, and movies, too, enlarge our repertoire. Or they allow unrealized possibilities that were in us all along to find some vehicle for expression. There is a kind of vision that some directors have—Fellini or Antonioni or Bergman or Kurosawa—that we can carry with us out into that harsh daylight. More often, it is a set of facial expressions, speech patterns, and bodily postures—Bogart's or Cagney's or Brando's or Pacino's or George Sanders'—that imprint themselves upon us and become a part of our neural landscape.

James Stewart never played bad guys. My recollection is that his wife didn't want him to do this, and he was afraid that it would taint his on-screen image. Henry Fonda was, almost always, a good guy. But Sanders was not so constrained, and he had either the courage or the *grande indifference* to play villains, particularly if they were stylish villains, with just a touch of Oscar Wilde elegance to them. Like Claude Rains or Adolphe Menjou or James Mason, he could accept and exemplify more of the range of human experience. His elegance not only softened what would otherwise have been too unpleasant but also expressed a kind of sadness, which was what Rossellini saw in him. It is the fastidiousness that doesn't quite counterbalance the villainy and leaves him always with some degree of dejection. There is a part of Addison DeWitt that is as much offended by what he is doing as we are.

★

It is for these almost unspoken reasons, these irrational feelings of projection, incorporation, or connection, that there are fans, paparazzi, gossip magazines, and shows like *Entertainment Tonight*. The lives of these movie actors do not matter to any of us, any more than the fortunes of our local teams, but we imagine through them a larger and more intense connection to the world than what our jobs, our hobbies, and our family life can provide. It is painful to acknowledge such a muddle, but dishonest not to, and Sanders, Conway, Zsa Zsa, and the rest persist in the ether, not quite so vividly as my parents do or some of my departed friends, but with a much greater complexity and immediacy than I might have expected. The Greeks were right about how some figures are memorable and are heroes who, at their deaths, are transformed to become sacred springs or are promoted to the heavens to shine as stars.

7

HIS PRIVATE LIFE, AS HE RECOUNTS

it in his autobiography, was pleasant enough. He had Albert, his butler, taking care of him attentively. (Not Piotr or Vladimir?) As Sanders reports, "Albert was an excellent cook and knew how to do all the things around the house that wives do, except of course the only thing for which women are indispensable. But in regard to the latter the bachelor has no problems. On the contrary, he has over the married man the not inconsiderable advantage of infinite variety."

Let us take him at his word and assume that he got laid a lot. It is what his on-screen character would have done. And he was a movie star, after all. I am reliably informed that back in his "bachelor days," Warren Beatty would sidle up to one attractive woman or another on those studio tours and whisper in her ear, "You want to fuck a movie star?

It'll take twenty minutes." He got turned down some, but he got a lot of acceptances. The terms of the deal were clear enough, and he, and it, were attractive.

But the variety Sanders speaks of pales and palls, and the starlets begin to blur together. Otherwise, it is impossible to explain how happy he seems to have been to settle down with Benita Hume Colman, Ronald Colman's widow, and as he says in a non-snide observation in his autobiography, "On the whole I must say that I look upon Benita as the best thing that has happened in my life."

No, make that more energetic. Colman died in 1958 of emphysema. And Sanders, with whom Colman had not been particularly close and of whom he had even rather disapproved, immediately began courting Benita. Their relationship for twenty years had been an odd one in which Benita was forever finding Sanders women who might be suitable matrimonial candidates, a kind of flirtation at one remove. And once Colman was out of the way, there was no reason for the remove. The Ahernes paid a condolence visit to Benita and were stunned by her announcement that she was thinking about marrying Sanders. "He's in Spain," Benita told Aherne, "on that picture with Ty Power [*Solomon and Sheba*]. He has been telephoning and writing to me every day. He is absolutely insistent. And d'you know, I'm half inclined to do it."

This is hardly consonant with Sanders' description of the pleasures of bachelor living, which was more a part of his screen persona, evidently, than of his experience in real life. The following February, they were married at the British Embassy in Madrid, and they remained happily married until Benita's death from bone cancer, in 1967.

For those eight years, Sanders seems to have been happy, which is, in literature, less interesting than misery. Freud says that we are happy (or "ordinarily unhappy" as opposed to hysterically miserable) if we are okay with ourselves in love and work. Evidently Sanders was content. This is not a state that requires much in the way of intellectual or spiritual resources. Those come more into play, I fear, when times are bad. Sanders was having a good run, or good enough, and he was able to enjoy it.

The movies he made during this period are not interesting. He does a caricature of himself most of the time—as Peter Lorre had resigned himself to doing. Lorre, with whom Sanders had appeared in a couple of Mr. Moto movies, had more fun, I think, in these campy exercises in self-parody, because he was in on the joke and managed to wink at us from behind the quirks and tics he affected—in *Beat the Devil,* most impressively, but also in those Roger Corman movies like *Tales of Terror* or *The Raven.* Sanders' appearance in Blake Edwards' *A Shot in the Dark* with Peter Sellers comes close to this genial fooling around, but it wasn't so clearly a joke for him to appear with Terry-Thomas in *Operation Snatch* or Buddy Hackett in *The Golden Head* or Sonny and Cher in *Good Times*. What we're talking about here is earnest, unmistakable, 24-carat dreck.

It's a living. And if one's life is elsewhere, it is tolerable. I left *Newsweek* in 1965. I had been happy enough there, but I had been there for seven years, which seemed like a nice biblical span. And I had just turned thirty, which was a reminder to me, if not of my mortality, then at least of the fact that I was now more or less a grown-up. And I had to ask myself whether this was how I wanted to spend my life.

Did I want to be on that platform of the White Plains railroad station when I was Crowther's age and going to see a movie? It was okay for me to be doing this now, but at a certain point it would begin to be slightly shameful to see him doing it, too. My parents were horrified. I'd found a job where all I had to do was go to the movies, and they were unable to understand why this was too strenuous for me. I told them that it wasn't strenuous but it was wearing to the spirit. They had worked too hard to get me the best education that America offered, maybe the best there was in the world at that time, and what was I doing with it? At a certain level, I knew they shared my feelings, because when my father spoke about me to his friends, he told them with some pride that I was at *Newsweek* but never mentioned that what I did there was write about the movies. He said I was an associate editor, which was true enough but left the erroneous impression that I was covering politics or business or international affairs. Something of importance and gravitas.

They were unwilling to concede this to me, though, because they had lived through the Depression and were cautious souls. This wasn't the thirties, however, but the sixties now, and I was brash and optimistic. "Yalies don't starve," I told them. They thought I was being impertinent, and of course I was.

Impertinence, though, is probably a basic part of the equipment of any movie reviewer. One needs to be arrogant, impertinent, and unimpressed by the wealth and power of the studios. We weren't allowed to go on junkets and accept favors from the studios (well, maybe lunch, but nothing more elaborate). But we were supposed to go to screenings. And what if the screening is on a chartered plane that is going to Las Vegas, as happened with *Come Blow Your Horn*? And then, at the end of the movie, when the plane landed and you found yourself there in Las Vegas, a "guest of Mr. Sinatra" at the Sands, what can you do except use the room, eat the food, drink the booze, and gamble a little? I never worried too much about that kind of thing, because I didn't think of it as important enough to take into account when I was writing my review. It doesn't take a lot of nerve to accept such a trip and then write an unfavorable notice. (Indeed, what takes character is to notice that the movie isn't at all bad and write favorably about it.)

I don't remember having actually spoken with Sinatra, which might have diminished him for me and turned him into a mere human. But I do recall that he had a guy following him around all the time with a thick sheaf of crisp uncirculated banknotes. Sinatra didn't like to touch used money. So the guy would take whatever bills were being tendered to his boss and exchange them for virginal currency. (Piotr-ish, maybe?)

My other tidbit about him is that I once heard from somebody who'd heard it from Ava Gardner that sex with Frank was very much a push-and-squirt affair. But then, ex-wives are not always reliable reporters, are they?

I had been offered my choice in 1963 of the books department or the movies desk, and I chose movies because I'm not a fast reader. But I'm a serious reader, and to confront a book and then report on it to an audience that mostly won't read the book (we had seven million readers, remember, and few books get that kind of an audience) meant that your review was a paragraph saying what it was, a paragraph saying who the author was, a couple of quotes giving the flavor of the book, and maybe an observation about how this fit in and why it was or wasn't important. And then a clever kicker, so the reader would be signaled that the experience had been completed. For a while, we even had a "Summing Up" bit, which meant a line and a half (the lines were thirty-nine characters long, I still remember) that was a smart-ass aide-mémoire. For people too busy to read the whole review, or who had read it but couldn't remember what they'd read. If you are going to treat some work of art, which some books are, with that kind of brusque disrespect, you're going to feel bad most of the time. Treating movies disrespectfully, who suffers? Not the movie, not the readers, and at least for a good long time, not you.

One can suggest something of the flavor of a book, which is written in words, in a book review, which is also in words. But a movie is written in light and noise, and it manipulates people and objects that appear to be real. Go review a hurricane, or a volcanic explosion, or a raging fire. All these things happen in movies, and there isn't a whole lot to say about them. You can talk about the cutting or the angles or the color, but you feel like a dope, a *feinschmecker* criticizing a view of mountains or a sunset. Movies are at the same time huge and beside the point. The late Robert Thom, a screenwriter who had been, like me, a student of Paul Weiss' at Yale, explained it succinctly to that philosopher and is quoted in his very interesting *Cinematics* (Southern Illinois University Press, 1975):

> Film is not an art and probably never will be. It may, however, be more important than art. It is history of unprecedented accuracy, and it makes history. It has revolutionized the world. It has changed the very character and function of politicians and statesmen— as well as wiping out one kind of universal naïveté forever, replacing it, perhaps, with a more dangerous and volatile naïveté. This it has done everywhere, in all countries, under all forms of government. It is to be compared to the invention of the wheel and of the printing press. . . . Film will never be worthy of comparison with a Rembrandt. But it may make the adventures of Gandhi, Roosevelt, and Lenin seem trivial. Depression, flood, famine and fire, personal desires, ambitions, goals—all will be and have been shaped by it. No monk spends more time at his prayers or meditations than our children do before filmed television. . . . Film is Pandora's box. When we enter the world of film, we are truly in the dark.

I never knew Thom. Like him, I had been a Scholar of the House at Yale, and I knew about him from Weiss. I followed his career with some interest. And sadness. He won an Emmy (with Reginald Rose) for an episode of *The Defenders* in 1963. The only film he wrote that anyone has ever heard of is *All the Fine Young Cannibals.* He never really hit it big, and he died in 1979. In Malibu, where Joanne Woodward's flocked VW was roaring up and down the highway.

The closest we ever came was that my ex-wife once sent me to a PTA meeting at Madame Correa's École Française in New York, where our son was in kindergarten. He'd been bringing back a lot of pictures that were all in black, and my ex-wife was worried that this might be a sign of severe psychological disturbance. (She had been reading Melanie Klein!) She didn't want to have to compete with the other mothers, like Sybil Burton, whose daughter Katie was in my son's class, and Janice Rule (who had been married to Thom for about a year and was sending her daughter—probably not Thom's, but the one she had with Ben Gazzara—to the École). So I was the one to go. Paul Weiss said many times that Rule was the most beautiful woman he'd ever seen—and she was surely up there, in anyone's book. I thought about introducing myself, mentioning Weiss, and Thom of course. But I had no idea if this would be awkward or even painful for her. So I just carried out my assigned task. (It turned out that there was only one pot of black paint, and it went as a prize to whoever was the fastest cleaner-upper after naptime. Evan was a whiz, was very competitive, and would have valued the paint for its scarcity. So, he wasn't screwed up after all, only an economist-to-be.)

But Thom was right about movies. They are beyond not only analysis but even comprehension. To look at them professionally requires, as I've suggested, brashness. And also a free-floating attention. My friend Richard Dillard taught a course in movies at Hollins College (now University) in Roanoke, and one of the questions on the exam asked the students to describe the scene in each film they had seen that had a chicken in it. And he'd set it up so that there was at least one brief glimpse of a chicken in each of the films they'd studied. But he never made any mention of this or referred to it in any way. Unfair? Of course. But a very good gauge, nonetheless, as to the quality of attention the students had brought to the experience of the film.

A free-floating attention that notices things in the movies and around the movies, where much of the reality lies anyway. For instance, Paul's notion about Janice Rule. Do I really agree? My vote, I guess, would go either to Claudia Cardinale or Romy Schneider. But I am willing to defer to real expertise. My friend George Garrett, coming back from a year on a Prix de Rome, was on the *Michelangelo* with his family in cabin class. It was noisy in the cabin and less than luxurious in the public rooms. He found that if he made an appointment with the masseur, he could go up to first class, have a massage, and then on the way back, stop at the first-class bar and sit and drink until somebody noticed him and threw him out. At which point he'd make an appointment for another massage. He got to know the masseur pretty well. There wasn't a masseuse on the boat. This guy did everybody. And George asked him who had the best body of all the Italian movie stars. Without hesitation, the masseur said, "Rossana Podestà. Such muscle tone!"

One must bear that kind of thing in mind—as I have now for years. It's up there with the remark I once heard from Robert Penn Warren to the effect that one should, at least once in a lifetime, make love with a woman who rode horses. "The thigh muscles are wonderfully well developed," he said. Poetry, they say, is memorable speech, and that qualifies.

But these women are not merely pinups. The fondness Weiss had for Janice Rule was partly informed by the fact that he knew her. She and Robert Thom must have come to visit him once or twice. And my recollection of Romy Schneider is lit by the memory of our having breakfast together in her room at the Plaza, where she or her publicist had arranged our interview. Intentionally or not (and I've considered both possibilities and don't care), her robe kept falling open to reveal quite a lot of leg.

And I affected not to notice. And she affected not to observe my refusal to react. It was, within very narrow constraints, a relationship. Relationships are also what we form with the creatures on-screen, in whom we invest emotions and whose looks are an essential part of that transaction. Oddly, an actress who is less than drop-dead gorgeous (Judi Dench, Meryl Streep, Helen Mirren) can do other things, like act, without the dazzling beauty getting in the way.

8

LEAVING THE MAGAZINE WORKED

out well, better than I could have expected. But it has had its ups and downs. I have done some good work of which I'm proud. And I've done some dumb things, the big money novels I used to be able to turn out (as Henry Sutton). The difference between Sanders and me was mostly that when I was doing something good, I generally knew it was good and could enjoy it, which wasn't the case with him.

What would have been even worse, I suppose, would have been the knowledge that he'd done something truly fine that had been a commercial failure, ignored or rejected by a not very smart public. This was what happened to Kirk Douglas, with whom I had lunch once, and I was foolhardy enough to ask him about Stanley Kubrick's *Paths of Glory*, which was a sore subject. His chin dimple deepened, and he told me what a great film it was and, in his rage at its disappointing reception, actually broke the wineglass in his hand, so that the waiter had to bring a napkin to staunch the bleeding.

Sanders, so far as I am able to intuit, had no such great investment in the movies. His connection was to the character, which was mostly the same, an idealized projection of himself. I think it was Freddie Raphael who told me that he'd once asked Mastroianni how it was that he could so cheerfully play cowards, men who were impotent, and other sorts of unflattering roles. Mastroianni smiled and said, "Beh, they're only movies." Sanders didn't connect any more intimately with the films he made but with the figure of himself up on the screen—in which he believed too much.

I had heard that dismissal of movies before, in different circumstances and with a different accent, from Alfred Hitchcock. His press agent had arranged for me to interview him at breakfast in his hotel the morning after I'd seen the film at a press screening. The movie was *The Birds*, and I hated it. A lot of technical dazzle that couldn't retrieve an essentially stupid story. It has Rod Taylor and Tippi Hedren in it, and I never much liked either of them. Taylor always seemed to have been carved by Northwest Coast Indians out of wood. And Tippi Hedren sounded like the name of a PMS medicine. Also Suzanne Pleshette—but I didn't hate the movie just because she was in it. The story itself, that the birds revenge themselves on people and take over Bodega Bay, was just barmy. And uninvolving. So I told the press agent (whose name, after all these years, escapes me) that he should cancel the breakfast. It would be unpleasant for both of us.

He called me at home later that evening. This in itself was weird. Nobody calls a critic at home! And what he told me was weirder—that he'd be fired, that he and his children would be out on the street, that I should do this as a personal favor, that Hitchcock knew I'd disliked the movie and didn't care. Please, for God's sake, come to breakfast.

It's Hitchcock, remember. A great moviemaker. And a kind of frightening guy. Would he put strychnine in my coffee? I agreed that I'd go. And I showed up on time at the St. Regis, where Hitch opened the door himself and said, "I understand you didn't like the film. But that's all right. It's only a movie. Come in. Have breakfast. We'll talk."

He'd used the line before, of course, but it was charming. The breakfast was fine. And the information about how many cuts there had been in the scene with the birds collecting on the jungle gym was mildly interesting. But I took the man at his word, remembered that it was only a movie, and panned it. The only thing I regret is that he'd neglected to tell me that they fed the birds a combination of wheat and whiskey to make them manageable and get them to stand still. It would have been lovely to throw that in somewhere in the review.

★

I like to think that Sanders had a good time during those years he spent with Benita and could feel okay about himself, because there were offers and paychecks, and even when he was doing dopey movies, he had a technical competence in which he could take some pride. He could enunciate, stand here, move there, sneer dependably . . . he could show up. And frankly, if, during this time, he'd had a heart attack or come down with cancer or had been hit by a truck, he wouldn't be so interesting to me. It's the thrashing around at the end, the desperation and the altogether out-of-character fear that I find riveting.

Ghoulish of me? Maybe so, but we look to other lives, those we know or can make guesses about, and try to infer from them some hints about how we might cope, ourselves, with the difficulties and diminutions most of us face, sooner or later. Happiness and contentment are wonderful, but they don't have much to teach us. Misery, I am afraid, is what's instructive.

Sanders had plenty of that. He had been trying to find ways to convert his movie money into something more reliable that wouldn't require him to stand in front of cameras, posing and sneering and delivering dim lines from grade-B scripts. He invested in Swiss real estate, Canadian oil wells, and a sausage company in Brighton. It is impossible to tell, but it would seem that Sanders was more the victim than the perpetrator of what turned out to be a swindle. In any event, in Los Angeles in October 1966, Sanders filed for bankruptcy, asking for the discharge of more than a million dollars. He claimed to have lost some $360,000 and had total assets of just under $58,000. In Britain, there was an investigation—the Royal Bank of Scotland had lent his company nearly half a million pounds to set up a farm to supply pork to the sausage company—and the report was grim, saying, "We do not accept his [Sanders'] claim to have been an innocent tool in the deceptions" and that "his behavior was . . . indifferent to the point of recklessness to the truth or untruth of statements in which he acquiesced."

One of Sanders' partners was arrested in California, charged with counterfeiting, and sent to jail.

This would be an embarrassment for anyone, but for Sanders, a person who had been playing that superior and knowing character on-screen, it must have been intolerable. The whole idea of the suave, sophisticated, assured, cynical address and elocution he had perfected was to project knowingness. He was not a bumpkin or a fool, knew the world, and could spot a cad or a bounder, because he had more than a touch of caddishness about him. But that assurance, that wardrobe with those elegantly tailored sport coats and suits, had taken him in, too, and he discovered that he was as innocent as Pa Kettle come to the big city to be fleeced by the slickers. This was out of "character." Of all the movie characters to be taken for such a ride, who could be less likely and, therefore, more humiliated?

Benita, meanwhile, was suffering terribly from arthritis and, as it turned out, also from bone cancer, from which she died in 1967.

Tony Thomas reports, in his epilogue to the 1992 reprint of *Memoirs of a Professional Cad,* that shortly before her death Sanders had an offer to do a big movie, but he turned down the part, Dr. Zaius in *Planet of the Apes,* saying, "After all I've gone through, I don't know that I'm emotionally capable of playing an ape."

Perhaps worse was that when she died, his Sanders persona seems to have prevented him from showing—and perhaps even from feeling—the sorrow he felt. To his friends he put on a stoic and even debonair face and said that Benita would not have wanted friends to grieve for her. That dapper blazer had become a straightjacket. And the constraints were driving him crazy.

He wasn't flat broke, maybe, but he was reduced to ordinariness. He needed the income from acting in order to live. And he was aging and ailing, so that the long-term prospects were increasingly dim. And even if he could fight time and stay just the same, there were fewer and fewer roles for his kind of character. Movies are no longer an entertainment for adults. The target audience is teenagers. Lorre and Karloff and even Vincent Price had figured out a way to earn a few dollars being laughed at, but that was just a little out of Sanders' range. And not at all to his taste.

Noël Coward had once said of Sanders, "He has more talents than any of us, but he doesn't do anything with them."

And now look at him! What the hell has happened?

I interviewed Coward once. Sir Noël, but he hadn't yet been knighted. He was, I am afraid, afraid of me. More clearly, he was afraid that I might take some terrible shot at him for being a homosexual. People did that then. I was a kid from *Newsweek*, which meant that I had a lot of readers but didn't necessarily know anything. I came up to his hotel room, and he was very stiff, very guarded, and grudging with his responses. I admired his loafers—the first Gucci loafers I'd ever seen with those gold buckles with the *G*s on them. At some point, he dropped some Coward line, working it into the conversation somehow. "Life called to Mrs. Wentworth-Brewster," it could have been. I came up with the next line, "Said *scusi*, and abruptly goosed her." And he flashed a tight smile, because now he knew that I might be a fan, might know at least a little, and could perhaps be trusted in a cautious way, so he opened up and talked to me some.

Only later did I realize how horrible this was, that a man like that, whom I very much admired, should have to worry about someone like me.

They worry. They all worry. Ned Rorem once told me that, from the outside, these lives look like one success after another, but that's because from the outside nobody can see the failures, the rejections, the slights and bruises.

Now, even from the outside, Sanders wasn't looking so good. And whether or not he had read James Joyce's short stories, he was smart enough to be aware of what was happening to him.

When I meet young writers, they assume that I have it made. They look at all those books—nearly ninety, now—and assume that it's easy for me. They don't know how to read a bibliography. I'm like one of those actors who can't get work in the studios, so I am out there with the independents doing art films, or in literary terms, with the university presses, which pay a lot less.

I don't blame anyone. That's how it is. Gertrude Stein said that in the eighteenth century, nobody could make a living as a writer, because not enough people knew how to read; in the nineteenth century, you could make a living as a writer; but in the twentieth century, you can't make a living as a writer, because too many people know how to read.

In a time when Imus and Oprah are the two most influential people in bookselling, there's no place left for literature. The university presses? They hang on, but just barely, foraging on the leavings of the trade houses. You suppose that they'd get subsidies from the universities, because scholars need to publish in order to get promoted, and the presses are a vital part of that process. But no, nothing that sensible. Here and there, a few universities let their presses off without charging them rent. But they have to break even. Otherwise, like Northeastern University Press, they are closed down—which turns Northeastern into a pretentious community college, actually.

I can't tell whether it was better or worse for Sanders. He never had the solace of knowing that the work he was doing was good, but that kind of knowledge can be a burden, and within reason, the less admirable projects didn't oppress him. He even had to be aware that he was mostly doing bits, small character parts, and cameos, in on-the-cheap productions of no interest either artistically or commercially. What I think was most bothersome to him was the lack of control, the utter inability he must have felt to change anything, to improve anything in either his performances or in the roles and deals he was offered.

The descriptions on the credits are often misleading. Some actors have enormous power. Since the collapse of the old studio system, they have become even more important and are often the basis of the financing. But even in the old days, some stars could throw their weight around. Mary Pickford and Douglas Fairbanks used their directors like butlers. In *The Merry Widow*, Mae Murray came back every night to reshoot her close-ups after Erich von Stroheim had left the set and the studio. Murray made sure that Louis Mayer and Irving Thalberg saw the versions that she liked, and many of her contributions were in the final film. If I know about these things—and I am an observer, a dabbler—then Sanders must have known hundreds of such stories. And even in the best of times, he never had that clout. When the rest of his life was okay, that probably didn't bother him much, but as things began to fall apart, he would have wanted to do something, to fix it, to recoup, and there were no options. The whole situation is one that could have knocked a sturdier fellow off his pins. Or to put it more clinically, I see Sanders in his last years as depressed. Zsa Zsa's book—*Zsa Zsa Gábor, My Story, Written for Me by Gerold Frank*—mentions that Sanders usually slept twelve hours a night and quipped about it, "Obviously an escape, my dear. I'm trying to find out from what."

Aherne mentions, en passant, a Dr. Theodore Rothman, who had been Sanders' psychiatrist "for many years," which suggests that there was something troubling him. And his suicide? That's what depressed people, or some of them anyway, do. This is, a shrink friend of mine informs me, all the more likely where there is substance abuse, drugs or alcohol, and Sanders was using a lot of both of them. And that was why Dr. Rothman would have had reason to worry.

He was lonely now, not just a Sanders-like bachelor but a widower, who had been happy with Benita, who had enjoyed connubial companionship, the coziness of a marriage, and now was hideously bereft of the multitude of minor blessings one can find in being in an us-against-the-world partnership.

That, I rather think, is what drove him into the frenzy Aherne reports, that altogether cuckoo idea about going to Mexico, marrying Dolores Del Rio, and running for the presidency of Mexico. Well, to be fair, he and Del Rio had starred in a couple of films thirty years before—*Lancer Spy,* which I have never seen but which looks to be not too terrible and has Peter Lorre in it, and *International Settlement,* which I haven't seen either and which is apparently less good. But give him the benefit of the doubt and assume that he and Del Rio had an affair back then or, more crudely, found themselves in bed together a few times. That's enough to allow at least for the fantasy of recovering a lost youth, reviving an old romance to which the passage of time has given an attractive patina, and reclaiming a woman he thinks of, somehow, as "his." So the idea of seeing Del Rio isn't, on its face, absurd. Even marrying her, even for her money, isn't altogether nuts. But the presidency of Mexico? That has a memorable dottiness that goes back to rival that of old Uncle Sasha.

At least Sanders knew where Mexico was. Zsa Zsa, in her account of her meeting with Rubirosa, confesses that she had no clear idea of the location of the Dominican Republic. As far as she was concerned, it could have been one of those invented Ruritanias that movies are supposed to happen in.

"Hail to Freedonia, land of the brave and free!"

In her romanticized and self-serving account of the night she began her affair with Rubirosa at the Plaza, she asks us to believe that Sanders was psychic and that, after the very night in which she and her polo-playing diplomatic stud were romping on the bed for the first time, she awoke to find a cable from Sanders—sent perhaps at the very moment of intromission?—that had been left at her door: AM IN LONDON I MISS YOU TERRIBLY I LOVE YOU I LOVE YOU GEORGE.

It's easy enough to dismiss. It's Zsa Zsa, after all,

and she is full of shit. But who is to deny that God has his moments of tacky sentimentality too?

Sanders was thinking of her, maybe not continuously but from time to time. Like Ms. Del Rio, she had money, maybe not so much as Sanders would have liked to believe, but some. She had that house in Bel Air. She had that settlement from Conrad Hilton. She had the money from those television and nightclub appearances. (What in hell could she have done in a nightclub?) She says in one of her autobiographies that she was making two hundred thousand dollars a year, although she adds that she was spending a lot of that. But from Sanders' point of view, that was comfortable. (She has less now, I'm afraid, having been one of Bernie Madoff's victims.)

He and Zsa Zsa had worked together in *Death of a Scoundrel,* got on together well enough, and were amicable, even, perhaps, intimate, for old times' sake. Why not?

So it was likely that, a decade later, in his illness, his financial worry, and his generally bleak mood, he might have had idle notions about remarrying her. She was funny. "Amusing," to use the standard Rossellini's Alex Joyce finds congenial. And she could take care of him, which is something married people do for each other. The chances of her disappearing to carry on with a Rubirosa were now diminished. If she wanted to hump a pool boy, fine, so much less for Sanders to have to do himself. But there would be someone with whom to have breakfast. A lawn on which to play croquet. And an end to the panic he was feeling about how to face the demands and threats of the future.

The more he thought about it, the less silly it seemed. (After the presidency of Mexico, almost any idea is going to seem more plausible.) He invited Zsa Zsa to dinner in Beverly Hills and proposed to her.

Her answer—that he should marry her sister Magda instead—surprised him.

What? Was this a joke? Apparently not. As Aherne recounts his telephone conversation with Sanders, Zsa Zsa was absolutely serious—or as serious as any Gabor can be about anything other than jewelry. She explained that it would be a wonderful arrangement, and they could take care of each other—Magda had also, apparently, had a bad fall from which she was recovering slowly. But she also had a lovely house in Palm Springs. And it would be such a pleasure to have him back in the family! This, we can assume, she delivered with her usual come-hither purr, suggesting somehow that she might throw herself in for an occasional romp with her ex-husband, who would now be her brother-in-law.

Magda's willingness to be involved in such an arrangement was not even a question. She had been married before, to Jan de Bichovsky, a pilot in the RAF who may or may not have been a Polish count, to William Rankin, to Sidney Warren, and to Tony Gallucci, from whom she had been divorced three years before. Sanders would be the fifth. If you add up all the marriages of all three Gabor sisters, you get nineteen, which is impressive.

Why not? It could do all that Zsa Zsa was promising. It was a bit part. But he was getting used to that, these days.

Perhaps the real attraction was that he could not easily imagine it. In order to find out what it would be like, he'd actually have to do it.

So? So . . . sure!

But, no, I think it was worse than any of that. I think what moved him to do it was that it was like one of his movies; it was in character; it was consistent with the dumb parts he'd been playing for all those years in all those mostly trashy movies, which, after a while, he began to take seriously. There wasn't any offscreen person, or if there was, then it was a pitiable figure he didn't want to be. It was a way of signing on to a project where somebody else—Zsa Zsa, in this case—would be telling him where to move, where to look, what to say, what mark to get his feet on. Familiar, reassuring. And, most of the time, these movies have happy endings, don't they?

Is that a way to think about life?

But then, for most of us, is there a better way?

It was a fiasco and lasted less than a week. She had money, but that, it turned out, was the problem. He wasn't Sanders-ish enough, was much less suave and unprincipled than the adventurer he played in movies, and, as it turned out, hated having to ask for money "every time he went into town."

He and his for-the-moment wife visited the Ahernes, driving a white Cadillac, which, if it wasn't the big Bentley of *Viaggio*, would, at that time, have had the same boatlike aspect. Magda was still recovering from the fall and could speak only with difficulty. But she made it clear that she didn't want a divorce, would be ashamed at so public a failure. (A Gabor? Ashamed? Was that even in their repertoire?)

Aherne asked how it would be possible to get a divorce so soon after the marriage, but Sanders had an answer ready, a more reasonable one, this time, than his scheme of avoiding taxes by living on a houseboat in the middle of the Rio Grande: they could get an annulment within two weeks of the marriage, under California law, if they both signed a declaration that he was impotent.

"Oh, George, no!" Aherne quotes Magda as wailing.

But which is worse? Was the declaration a legal

fiction? Or was it true? Had there been occasion even for them to find out?

Magda was the reluctant one in this transaction, but it was Sanders who should have been. It amounted to nothing less than a death sentence, not quite for him but for the dream he'd had of independence from the movies, of the good life, of the pool, the croquet games, the smoking jackets and the cigars, if not footmen with jam pots and champagne. But now he had to worry about getting by, the way most of us do. And the prospects were dismal. Prospects are often more important than one's present condition. People will put up with almost anything (an internship, basic training) if they are convinced that it will be better later. But when there is no hope of improvement, or worse, when there is a certainty of disimprovement, what you get is misery. Whether it crept up on him or he realized it abruptly, he saw that he was deteriorating and would continue to do so.

I had some ice cream a month or so ago and, in a "senior moment," put the ice cream container back, but not in the freezer. Inadvertent, vague, I put it in the refrigerator, where, of course, it melted.

My wife thought it was funny. I didn't.

Sanders didn't have a wife to tell him that it was funny. Or to reassure him that it wasn't what he generally did, or at least not yet.

That image of him chopping up his piano with an axe is dismal and depressing. The next scene, the one in the Hotel Don Jaime, is, for us as it was for him, a release and almost a relief.

But then, which is worse? To go out like that? Or to keep on living, increasingly powerless and diminished, married, like, say, Zsa Zsa to a joke prince who keeps getting his name—and therefore hers, too—into the tabloids? For Britney Spears or for Zsa Zsa's niece Paris Hilton, this is merely absurd. But for a grown-up? It's humiliating.

Sanders' speech was impaired and he was decaying physically. He wasn't going to get any better and knew it. And ending it seemed to him more attractive than pressing onward. He was depressed, but depressed people can make rational decisions. The playacting wasn't in the suicide, but in the note, which was dapper, the last vestige of that character he'd played for so long and of which he could not, even at the last, let go. Very Alex Joyce. Very Addison DeWitt. That was, by God, who he was, or at least the part he'd been playing to the world and to himself, even primarily to himself. That was the fellow he'd much rather be. And if going out was the way to validate the note, or if the note was the script for the scene, then he'd play it.

Figure it as a stylistic requirement. The genre of suicide notes is demanding that way. What sticks in the mind, what makes it not just the death of a movie star but a serious and revealing incident in our culture, is how style not only colors but actually prompts action. The assertion of style can shape reality, and if that's true, then we're into interesting philosophical and dramatic territory.

Of course, at the basic level, it was sad, as any suicide must be. Rossellini had seen that sadness in him and had used it in *Viaggio*. It is not unlike the richer melancholy of Mastroianni in *La dolce vita* or *8½*, an elegant and knowing vulnerability that is both painful and appealing. Sanders' performance there and in *All About Eve* earned him a crumb of immortality.

It's more than most of us get.